J. S. Mill: The Evolution of a Genius

J. S. MILL

The Evolution of a Genius

Peter Glassman

University Presses of Florida

UNIVERSITY OF FLORIDA PRESS / GAINESVILLE

Copyrighted material has been quoted from the following works:

Autobiography and Other Writings, by John Stuart Mill, edited by Jack Stillinger, Riverside Edition B117, published by Houghton Mifflin Company, © 1969 by Houghton Mifflin Company. Reprinted by permission of the publisher.

Collected Works of John Stuart Mill, edited by F. E. L. Priestley and John M. Robson, published by University of Toronto Press. Passages from the following volumes are reprinted by permission of University of Toronto Press and Routledge and Kegan Paul: *Earlier Letters of John Stuart Mill* (vols. 12, 13), © 1963 by University of Toronto Press; *Later Letters of John Stuart Mill* (vols. 14–17), © 1972 by University of Toronto Press; *Principles of Political Economy* (vols. 2, 3), © 1965 by University of Toronto Press.

The Early Draft of John Stuart Mill's "Autobiography," by John Stuart Mill, edited by Jack Stillinger, published by the University of Illinois Press, © 1961 by the Board of Trustees of the University of Illinois. Reprinted by permission of the publisher.

Essays on Politics and Culture, by John Stuart Mill, edited by Gertrude Himmelfarb, published by Doubleday & Co. Inc., © 1962 by Gertrude Himmelfarb.

On Liberty, by John Stuart Mill, published by W. W. Norton & Co., © 1975. Reprinted by permission of the publisher.

University Presses of Florida is the central agency for scholarly publishing of the State of Florida's university system, producing books selected for publication by the faculty editorial committees of Florida's nine public universities. Orders for books published by all member presses of University Presses of Florida should be addressed to University Presses of Florida, 15 NW 15th Street, Gainesville, FL 32603.

Library of Congress Cataloging in Publication Data

Glassman, Peter J., 1945–
  J. S. Mill: the evolution of a genius.

  Bibliography: p.
  Includes index.
    1. Mill, John Stuart, 1806–1873. 2. Philosophers—England—Biography. I. Title.
B1607.G57 1985   192 [B]   84–16286
ISBN 0-8130-0814-X (alk. paper)

Typesetting by G & S Typesetters, Austin, Texas.

Printed in the U.S.A.

To Nicholas Andrew Glassman
and Emily Catherine Glassman

CONTENTS

Preface   ix
Acknowledgments   xv
Introduction   1
1. The Childhood   7
2. Separation and Integration   49
3. Love and Marriage   88
4. Resolution and Independence   106
5. "Language and Manner":
   The Nature and the Uses of Authorship   121
6. 'Who Made Me?': The *Autobiography*   136
7. "One's Own Path Is Clear"   164
   Notes   169
   Bibliography   181
   Index   187

PREFACE

Psychoanalytic criticism is decidedly out of fashion. There are a number of explanations for the recent eclipse of a once valued critical mode. One is that many contemporary literary scholars have become interested in methods of criticism that focus extreme attention upon texts rather than upon authors. Another is that psychoanalytic criticism often has been practised by persons who are poorly trained or even untrained in psychoanalysis. The excesses of inept analysts perhaps have become associated with the method. The principal explanation, I believe, is that psychoanalysis itself has become increasingly mistrusted during the past several years. The conclusions of psychoanalytic theory, the methodologies of psychoanalytic therapy, and, above all, the multiple arrogances of many psychoanalytic therapists, critics, and biographers have created a strong sense of resentment among the lay community. There seems to be a widely shared belief throughout the contemporary culture that psychoanalysis oversimplifies and perhaps vulgarizes human emotions and behavior.

Many literary critics experience this belief and the irritations that

support it in an especially intense way. Many of my colleagues conclude that psychoanalysis drastically misrepresents the processes and
the meanings of imaginative thought. Many scholars argue that it is
most seriously inappropriate to treat a work of literature as a symp-
tomatology. It makes an offense against the autonomy of art, many
critics believe, to conceive of literature solely as an expression of its
maker's mentality. An author, it often is asserted, is ultimately discrete from or at least separable from his works. Writing literature
does not seem to these commentators to be really or merely a *behavior*. There occurs, it may be said, an inspiration in the making of art.
Many critics believe that the authorities of this indefinable but
powerful stimulation are crucial and wonderful; and that they are
inaccessible to psychoanalytic interpretation.

The ardency with which these views are felt and advanced may be
at least partially defensive. Like all other readers, critics transfer
many of their personal experiences, emotions, and desires onto the
literature they read. When we confront works of creative and critical
writing, we inevitably confront aspects of ourselves. I believe that
psychoanalytic interpretations have excited so much hostility among
more conventional scholars at least in part because psychoanalytic
methods expose readers' (and scholars') as well as authors' passions
and purposes. In literary criticism as elsewhere, ire frequently operates as an idiom of surprise, shame, and fear. Hostility often masks
recognition and panic.

Whether or not the contemporary reaction is partially hysterical,
modern critics surely are correct to insist that psychoanalysis must
not trespass against the complexity and the peculiar sovereignty of
creativity. Nevertheless, it must be apparent to everyone that authoring is *an activity*. However complex, however curious, imagining and inventing are behaviors. Like all other behaviors, they are
inevitably expressive to at least some extent of the emotions of the
person who is behaving.

The uncompromising hostility of criticism to psychoanalysis is
most unfortunate. Criticism and psychoanalysis should not be, they
cannot be, absolutely discriminable from one another. The two dis-
ciplines are branches of a single science: the science of human cognition. The insights that psychoanalysis makes it possible for us to
achieve are not dispensable to criticism. All of us who are critics of
literature must try to learn as much as can be known about the ori-

gins of imagination, the purposes of expression, and the meanings of language.

Arrogance and absolutism are another matter. Psychoanalysis and its practitioners must not affect to know everything about everyone. The founder of psychoanalysis never made such a claim. Serious and skilled psychoanalytic critics never make such a claim. Psychoanalysis can promote certain kinds of awareness about creative art and about creative artists. These discoveries can become included among other, equally insightful recognitions. Properly viewed and properly applied, psychoanalysis does not threaten criticism. Psychoanalysis merely supplies materials to criticism: materials that often can be of momentous importance.

In the discussion that follows, I consider as related phenomena the life and the literature of J. S. Mill. I try to demonstrate that Mill's experience and his reactions to his experience unconsciously dominated his behaviors as a philosopher and a literary artist. I try also to show that Mill's work as an artist eventually came to exercise authority upon his experience. To a considerable degree, Mill may have "written" his life; certainly, to a considerable degree, his experience authored his literature.

It is not my intention to expose or to scorn Mill as an ill man. I intend to suggest an opposite response. John Mill did suffer from severe disturbances and disorders. No wonder. His history was grotesque. What is startling and important about Mill was not his suffering but his resilience. Mill refused to capitulate to pain. He refused to submit to despair or to disease. In my essay I try to identify some of the major ways in which Mill combatted disablement. My purpose in writing the essay has been to celebrate as well as to analyze. Mill seems to me to be not a victim but a hero of modern civilization.

This is, then, a specialized study which has particular applications and purposes. I have not attempted to write a full biography of J. S. Mill. I have not written a biography of Mill's parents or a biography of Mill's wife. I have not written a critical study of his literature. As I hope my title indicates, I have attempted to trace some of the principal means by which Mill defined and fulfilled his character. I have tried to write a history of Mill's literary and psychological creativity.

I do not hesitate to declare that my methods are impressionistic and speculative. I treat Mill's literature, his diaries, his letters, and his preliminary manuscript drafts as texts of equal interest and authority. I consider the language that the author wrote as evidence of what the man thought, what the man felt, and what the man believed he needed. This will be and should be seen as a controversial practice. Writing is not by any means an analytic situation. An author's discourse surely differs substantially from an analysand's discourse. However, an author's literature in significant ways approximates or parallels an analysand's dialogue. Literature, like the narrative of an analysand, does not always flow from rationally calculated or logically mediated sources. All speech carries symbolic as well as discerned meanings. All uses of language express subliminal as well as supraliminal intentions.

It is possible, I believe, to apply to an author's work certain strategies of hearing and of interpreting that make it reasonable to attempt analytic conclusions. I believe that, with careful research and with sympathetic attention, an author's mentality may be asked to become a subject. I believe that, with much effort to be alert and with much effort to be reasonable, we may ask a writer's personal consciousness to become a part, perhaps a substantial part, of our appreciation and fascination.

This much I can promise my readers. I have tried to interpret responsibly. I have tried to adduce evidence for everything I have asserted. I have written "I believe" when I am expressing views that may be thought to be especially interpretive. I acknowledge that I interpret throughout this book. I acknowledge that my evidences are imperfectly conclusive. I may add that this seems to me quite generally to be the case in all works of critical investigation. Some modes of speculation are more concealed; but they are equally impressionistic.

I hope I have made it apparent that I regard my reading as a contribution, not a displacement. I hope that this book will contribute to our understanding of a man, of a phenomenon, and of a culture. Other ways of thinking about Mill, and other ways of writing biography and criticism, of course will retain their full validity and appeal. As Mill taught us so well, differing approaches to reasonable thought do not in any serious way threaten one another.

I hope that what I suggest about Mill's mind and its patterns will seem provocative and at least probably true. I am addressing in this book literary critics, psychoanalysts, historians of society, and all other persons who feel curious about the mysterious miracle of human creativity.

The Chinese University of Hong Kong
Sha Tin, New Territories
Hong Kong

ACKNOWLEDGMENTS

The American Council of Learned Societies awarded me a full year grant, which gave me time to develop this project and to become aware of its complexity. I am very grateful to the Council.

Chapter Six of this volume appeared in slightly different form in *Prose Studies*.

Professor Philip Dodd of the University of Leicester and Professor Albert A. Hayden of Wittenberg University gave me a great deal of assistance during the early stages of my work. I am grateful for their helpful advice.

Professor Bruce Mazlish of the Massachusetts Institute of Technology is as generous as he is learned and creative. His constant advocacy and splendid advice made it possible for me to write this book. I am also very happily indebted to Professor John D. Rosenberg of Columbia University. Professor Rosenberg's extensive criticisms and his extraordinary encouragement were of the greatest possible help to me.

My colleagues and students at the Chinese University of Hong

Kong have been a source of much inspiration. I am especially grateful to Professors Yuan Heh-hsiang, Chou Ying-hsiung, John J. Deeney, and Michael Holstein. Ms. Grace Shum must be the most patient and the most helpful secretary in Asia.

I am deeply grateful to Dr. Ann Price. Dr. Price helped me shape my mind; and she taught me much about the intricate assumptions and the healing power of psychoanalysis. I could not have written this book without her concern and care.

My brother, Dr. Andrew Glassman, and my sister Nancy Glassman believed in this work and helped me carry it forward. My father, James Glassman, and my stepmother, Robin Glassman, taught me everything I know about the devotion of truly loving parents. My sister Sallie Ann Glassman stood by me in dark times. I give her my loving thanks.

Ms. Karen K. C. Lam has formed my intelligence and my heart, and much about this book. I am most lovingly thankful.

My greatest obligations, and my most joyful, are to my son, Nicholas, and my daughter, Emily. They forebore with my preoccupation and my clutter. They inspired my interest in childhood and my faith in children. To them I offer this book, with my gratitude for their unfailing faith and their sacred support.

INTRODUCTION

Many contemporary readers find
it difficult to believe that J. S. Mill was once a beloved and an extraordinarily influential author. Outside the academic community, Mill
has little immediately identifiable importance in modern political,
economic, and philosophical thought. He has retained almost no
authority or prestige as a stylist. Among all his books, only *On Liberty* and the *Autobiography* continue to attract anything like a wide
audience. Even *On Liberty*'s audience is not general: the essay is read,
for the most part, by scholars and by students. Among all Mill's
writings, only the *Autobiography* continues to command considerable
popular interest. It appears that modern readers feel much more engaged by Mill's life than by his literature. We are drawn, it seems,
far more to Mill's personal history than to his philosophies, attitudes, and stylistics.

Part of the continuing interest in Mill's life has surely to do with
his life's grotesqueness. Mill's parents were peculiar people. His education was radically unusual. His early life was remarkably secluded,
confined, and pressured. His sufferings were extreme—so extreme

I

as to seem epical in their magnitude and in their significance. His adulthood may not appear to have been much more successful. Mill became a cerebral and seemingly a remote man. Many contemporary readers believe that Mill became almost inhuman, or perhaps even antihuman.

We recoil from Mill's experience, and we feel compassion for him. However, Mill's experience also presents itself as a kind of entertainment. The repressiveness of his circumstances; the eccentricity of the people who became important to him; the extremity of his deprivations and his sufferings; the severity of his neuroses: all this exercises, ultimately, a weird appeal. We react to Mill's life as we might to a legend or to a fairy tale. We find ourselves feeling interested in Mill because he appears to have been so fantastic a creature. At the least, we perceive him to have exhibited a series of seemingly irreconcilable contradictions. He was brilliantly intelligent, and yet almost naively innocent. He was exaggeratively rational, and yet deeply sensual. He was an oppressed and a manipulated child, but he became a most liberated and a most liberal man. His socialization was thoroughly abnormal, but he became a profoundly civilized person. We scarcely can help but conclude that Mill's life well might have made the matter of some mad and marvelous fiction: a novel by Dickens, perhaps, or a fragment from a Greek myth. For many readers, Mill's thought may have lost the power to compel. His history, though, remains intriguing.

I believe that it is precisely the actualness of the *Autobiography's* seemingly fictitious material that constitutes much of the work's singular appeal. Most readers seem to feel moved by the sheer historicity of the book's often strange and discomforting tale. Or rather, I believe, the sense of the real that we receive from the story of Mill's life simultaneously conflicts and conjoins with the spirit of the fictive. This collision between the reality of the actual and the impression of the imaginary is shocking and wonderful. The effect of reading the *Autobiography* is as unsettling and as exciting as if, for example, *Oedipus the King* were suddenly to disclose itself to be a purely documentary work. The *Autobiography* affects us so powerfully because it evokes the mood of the uncanny at the same moment that it expresses an infatuation with the nature and the claims of fact.

We feel especially interested, I believe, by the *Autobiography's* account of Mill's boyhood. As we read and become acted upon by the book, we cannot help but feel awed by the extent of Mill's victimization. We wonder if any other child ever has been so much levied upon by his parents. We wonder if any other child ever has suffered so much unreasonable interference; so much cruel and dehumanizing subordination; so much, as we may say, excessive and unnecessary estrangement from himself and from life. The *Autobiography* makes us understand that Mill was a deeply loved child. The work continually reminds us that few other fathers ever have given more to a child than James Mill gave to John. We also are led to recognize, however, that few fathers ever have damaged a son so gravely and, it must be said, so deliberately. The *Autobiography* causes us to feel similarly surprised and alarmed by Mill's relationship with his mother. We learn that Harriet Mill's absolute absence as a parent was almost as distressing and debilitating for John as his father's absolute presence. The portrait is anything but lovely. The *Autobiography* compels us to conclude that in the James Mill household, as in some subversive novel or nightmare, the normally sustaining experiences of love, family, and socialization occurred as a confounding series of interlocking conflicts. The life which the *Autobiography* records intrigues us in part because it frightens us. It forces us to think carefully about the specific ways in which the social phenomena and the imaginative structures that we most cherish may sometimes molest and even maim us.

The *Autobiography* commands our attention for another reason. I think that we admire the book because we admire its author's resilience. As we read the *Autobiography*, we come to believe that few other men ever can have been so severely infringed upon as John Mill habitually was. For Mill, we realize, the experience of living could hardly have seemed anything other than an unending sequence of encroachments and violations. Yet, unless we read the *Autobiography* very carefully indeed, we shall conclude that Mill's afflictions barely mattered to him. No matter how primally he was aggressed against, he seems almost never to have yielded either to pain or to anger. Mill was a harshly subjugated child. But the *Autobiography* indicates that as an adult he became thoroughly aware of his impulses, and comfortable about responding to their demands. Everything that Mill tells us about his early life makes us understand that his infancy and childhood tormented and infuriated him. But his book makes it clear that as a husband, a citizen, and an artist he developed great respect for other persons, and great affection for all the acts of living. We feel mystified and delighted by Mill's power to survive his difficult experience. We cannot comprehend but we admire his unlikely evolution into a human being who could care about, trust, and treasure life, other people, and himself.

Mill's remarkable buoyancy is of much more than merely passing interest. It occurs to us as we read the *Autobiography* that the work calls into question one of the most established and certainly one of the most onerous of contemporary persuasions. We normally believe that our characterological structures are determined by our early history. Particularly we believe that, as Norman O. Brown describes the principle, "a succession of infantile traumata must establish more than a predisposition to lifelong neurosis."[1] Mill's *Autobiography* seems to invalidate this disturbing law. I believe that the story of Mill's life fascinates us at least in part because it appears to provide us with an historical example of an instance in which an individual refused to accede to the inevitability of psychological "predisposition." It seems to be exactly the significance of the *Autobiography* that its author would not permit there to develop a "lifelong" interrelation between himself and his problematic infancy and youth. As we read the *Autobiography*, we come gradually to believe that Mill somehow canceled his "infantile traumata." We conclude that Mill so fervently yearned to become healthy that he simply refused to be ill. One of the reasons that the *Autobiography* attracts us so much is that it allows us to suppose that a human being may liberate himself from virtually any experience of deprivation and pain.

Mill's rehabilitation of himself is the more impressive and the more exciting because it occurred, apparently, as an act of logical will. The *Autobiography* seems to demonstrate that by purely rational means a man can win his way to whatever condition he intelligently desires. The book suggests that if a person powerfully enough wants to become capable and creative, he can conquer, or he at least can control, every irrational impulse—even the ultimately irrational impulse of wanting or needing to accept "lifelong neurosis." In this aspect of its intention and effect the *Autobiography* presents itself as a modern version of the *Odyssey*. The work records the voyage of a great and a distinctly contemporary adventurer who overcame any number of forbidding obstacles in his journey toward selfhood, citizenship, and home.

This is what it pleases us to believe. It should be sentimental, however, to interpret the meaning of either Mill's life or the *Autobiography* exclusively in this way. Mill was implausibly resilient. But he was far less elastic than he understood himself to be. If we read his literature carefully, we learn that his boyhood gravely damaged his imagination. We learn that his emotions, ideas, and behaviors became decisively but subliminally controlled by his "infantile traumata." As we study his writings we discover that in fact Mill devoted most of his formidable intelligence and energy to a lifelong effort to repair the injuries that his history imposed upon his mind.

Mill did not wish to know this truth about himself. Nor, I have tried to suggest, do his readers necessarily wish to know this truth. Author and reader share in the *Autobiography* a subconscious desire to conceal the reality of trauma and the reality of reaction. The writer and his audience want to believe that Mill's sensations and conduct became somehow independent of events—independent, in particular, of the event of pain.

The means by which Mill tries simultaneously to reveal and to disguise his psychology make my subject. The subject concerns fiction and falsity. I shall suggest that John Stuart Mill, the Victorian civilization's hero of rationalism and sincerity, survived his potentially crippling childhood by mythologizing his existence. I shall suggest that Mill's readers unconsciously accept both the mythologizing and the purposes which fuel it. Together, I shall contend, the artist and his audience weave one of the most appealing fantasies of the Victorian age: the fantasy that a person can reject unpleasant reactions to unpleasant phenomena; the fantasy that, by rational means, a man can create the sensibility that he desires. I shall conclude by proposing that, for Mill, this delusion became successful. I shall try to demonstrate that Mill eventually succeeded in contriving—in authoring—a mentality which he needed, but which the events of his life prevented him from spontaneously achieving.

To John Stuart Mill's imagination of himself, and to the experiences that threatened to distort it, I now shall turn.

—I have a strong determination at present to see what the power of education can do.

_____1

The Childhood

As we read the *Autobiography* and as we reflect upon its subject's peculiar and difficult life, we feel that we must ask, before all other questions, why Mill was educated in the manner that he was. What could James Mill have been thinking of, we wonder. How could he have supposed it appropriate to conceive of and to treat his brilliantly gifted child as he did?

James Mill explained his intentions and motives in a note that he wrote in July 1806. Some seven weeks after the birth of John, James wrote a, for him, ebullient letter to Sir William Forbes, a socially established and very wealthy friend whose wife recently had delivered an infant son. In his letter James defines the uses to which he means to put his paternity. He writes:

I intend to run a fair race with you in the education of a son. Let us have a well-disputed trial which of us twenty years hence can exhibit the most accomplished & virtuous young man. If I can beat you in this contest, I shall not envy you that you can have yours the richest. I know not how often I

may fall from my good resolves in this, as I do in most other
cases, but I have a strong determination at present to see
what the power of education can do.[1]

We recognize that this is an excited communication. And we recognize that the writer intends to amuse. Neither of these circumstances prevents us from realizing that the letter's language exposes a
number of curious attitudes and expectations. We cannot help but
notice, for example, how frequently and how vehemently James invokes the vocabulary of contention: "race," "trial," "beat," "contest,"
"envy." The creator of this belligerent and rather frightened prose
seems to inhabit a universe that is ordered by the consciousness of
competition and the fear of defeat. James repeatedly suggests that to
live is to be constantly confronted or challenged. He implies that
by begetting and training a son he may reply to and perhaps even
avenge his life's humiliations and failures. James believes, it appears,
that a father may raise a child in the ways and for the reasons that
one might hurl an epithet: to strike back at everyone and at everything that ever has affronted, confounded, or intimidated oneself.

The letter is notable, too, for the number of ways in which it
maintains that a son's destiny and meaning depend almost exclusively upon a father's "good resolves" and "strong determination."
Not once in the paragraph does James suggest that a mother may
affect her child's life. Nor does he once mention either his own or his
friend's child by name. He speaks only of "a son" and of "an accomplished & virtuous young man." Midway through the letter this
neutering and usurping system of reference becomes actively aggres-
sive. In the passage's third sentence the two sons are made to seem
grammatically interchangeable with the two fathers (James writes:
"If *I* can beat *you* . . ."). James appears to be suggesting that he
conceives of the two children as absolute surrogates for the two sires.
The infants are made to seem completely passive, entirely subordi-
nated symbolizations of their progenitors. In the paragraph's final
sentence the language becomes unequivocally appropriative. John,
who previously has been described as a selfless manifestation of his
parent, here is referred to as a mere "case" or instance, altogether
alike in structure and in significance, apparently, to "most other
cases" in the father's long, abstractive, and evidently joyless
experience.

James presumably could create these strange and unpleasant constructions because he assumed that his child never would desire or need to develop in an autonomous way. He apparently supposed that John perforce would agree to live as the "trial" or as the emblem of his parent's intellectual and spiritual prowess. This happy father seems to have written to his friend with so much exuberance because he thought that he stood on the point of fathering himself. James believed, it appears, that he could annex his son and make him into a less vulnerable, "more accomplished" version of himself.[2]

The *Autobiography* goes to great lengths to demonstrate how seriously James regarded his "well-disputed trial" with the universe. In one of the work's most well-known passages, Mill's feelings of tension and anger are evident. Mill comments:

> In the case of . . . myself, [James] exerted an amount of labour, care, and perseverance rarely, if ever, employed for a similar purpose, in endeavouring to give, according to his own conception, the highest order of intellectual education. A man who, in his own practice, so vigorously acted up to the principle of losing no time, was likely to adhere to the same role in the instruction of his pupil.

He continues:

> I have no remembrance of the time when I began to learn Greek. I have been told that it was when I was three years old. My earliest recollection on the subject, is that of committing to memory what my father termed Vocables, being lists of common Greek words, with their significance in English, which he wrote out for me on cards. Of grammar, until some years later, I learned no more than the inflexions of the nouns and verbs, but, after a course of vocables, proceeded at once to translation.[3]

Generations of readers have felt surprised and repelled by the enormity of James's demands upon his son. We feel astonished by how much Mill was required to learn. We feel amazed by how hard he was required to work. We feel horrified, too, by the *Autobiography*'s account of the principles that shaped this laborious "instruction."

Throughout the book, Mill makes it clear that his education was
never collegial or genuinely confrontational. His training always was
coercive and co-optative. James established subject matters and
opinions "according to his own conceptions." From the age of three,
John submissively received what was set before him. His pupilage
and his sonship seem to have consisted primarily of "committing to
memory" hosts of "significations" which were created by his parent
and which were abstruse, if not absurd, to himself. The whole extraordinary curriculum in literature, languages, mathematics, logic,
political science, economics. geography, history, psychology, and
rhetoric was like "Vocables"—was like Greek—to Mill. For years he
packed into his consciousness long "lists of words" that his father
"wrote out for [him]."

Often Mill was compelled to represent his father's philosophies
and philologies as his own. "In [our] frequent talks about the books
I read," he recalls, "[my father] used, as opportunity offered, to give
me explanations and ideas respecting civilization, government, morality, mental cultivation, which he required me afterwards to re-
state to him in my own words" (*Autobiography*, 7). These recitations
masqueraded as free inventions. But usually they were feats of rote.
Throughout his childhood, Mill's "own words" were concealed exercises in subordination and sublimation. "It would have been wholly
inconsistent with my father's ideas of duty," Mill wryly notes, "to
allow me to acquire impressions contrary to his convictions and feelings" (*Autobiography*, 27).

In his circumspect way, Mill makes it clear that his father's manner toward him was as abusive and wounding as his pedagogic
method.[4] In the paragraph to which I have referred, he speaks of
himself not as James's son but as his "pupil." Mill echoes and extends this odd, lovelorn locution in a number of other, progressively
more sad and resentful passages. He comments: "My father, in all
his teaching, demanded of me not only the utmost that I could do,
but much that I could not possibly have done" (*Autobiography*, 6).
He later adds:

> I was continually incurring his displeasure by my inability to
> solve difficult problems for which he did not see that I had
> not the necessary previous knowledge. . . . [He] was often,

and much beyond reason, provoked by my failures in cases where success could not have been expected. (*Autobiography*, 9, 19)

James apparently found it necessary to treat arguably the least stupid and the most diligent child who ever has lived as though he were unintelligent and lazy. In an early version of the *Autobiography*, Mill recalls: "My father continually told me [I was] like a person who had not the organs of sense. . . . He could not endure stupidity, nor feeble & lax habits, in whatever manner displayed, & I was perpetually exciting his anger by my manifestations of them." [5] "I was constantly meriting reproof," he remembers. "I was incessantly smarting under his severe admonitions" (*Autobiography*, 23).

Often James seems to have been actively cruel. Apparently he regularly taunted and excoriated his son for his predictable lack of "bodily dexterity or practical skill & contrivance" (*Early Draft*, 180). His father's unconscionable gibes and rebukes provoked a sense of pain and sorrow which remained vivid for Mill throughout his life. Mill rarely addressed the subject. But whenever he did, he wrote about his feelings in ways that permit us to perceive how acutely his parent's ridicule and "severe admonitions" made him suffer. In perhaps the most hurt and certainly one of the most angry passages he ever composed, Mill declares in one version of the *Autobiography*:

From the earliest time I can remember, he used to reproach me, and most truly, with a general habit of inattention, owing to which, he said, I was constantly acquiring bad habits, & never breaking myself of them; acting like a person devoid of common sense; & which would make me, he said, grow up a mere oddity, looked down upon by everybody, & unfit for all the common purposes of life. . . . Whatever qualities he, probably, had acquired without difficulty or special instruction, he seems to have supposed that I ought to acquire as easily: & bitter reproaches for being deficient in them, were nearly all the help he ever gave me toward acquiring them. (*Early Draft*, 180, 180n.)

"From [my father's] . . . intercourse with me," Mill grievingly and bitterly comments, "I could derive none but a very humble opinion of myself" (*Autobiography*, 21).

_____

Passages of the kind I have cited invite us to suppose that James was a monster. We may conclude that his system of education was not merely excessively demanding and excessively abstract but also heartless and even psychopathic. Mill, however, does not seem to have experienced these reactions. He rarely condemns his father. He often panegyrizes him for his "perfect candour, and the real worth of his method of teaching" (*Autobiography*, 19).[6] In particular he celebrates James for the loving intention of his "method of teaching." Throughout his account of his childhood, Mill speaks with excitement and gladness of the constancy, closeness, and high seriousness that characterized the relationship he shared with his father. He frequently indicates that the rigorous way of life to which he was subjected felt extremely pleasurable to him because it seemed an unmistakable indication—it seemed, indeed, the very substance and idiom—of his parent's regard for him. He apparently saw in his "dry and irksome studies" (*Autobiography*, 34) an incontrovertible demonstration of the fact that James was willing to grant him "an amount of labour, care, and perseverance rarely, if ever" conferred upon a son by a father. The gratifications that this unique involvement of sire with son generated for Mill, the deep subliminal appeal for him of the morning crams, the afternoon walks, the evening catechisms, the whole daily round of his intense and intricate relationship with his father, make one of the *Autobiography*'s most touching and most troubling subjects.

The subject is troubling because, despite his many formal avowals of satisfaction, Mill often reveals that his relationship with his father gravely disappointed and disturbed him. His comments to this effect are numerous in the *Autobiography*. But they are subtle in their expression, and almost always they are reluctant. Mill remarks, for example, that his father always "demanded" things of him. He observes that his father never encouraged or inspired him. He rather "required" or "made" him think, feel, undertake, and achieve (*Autobiography*, 6, 15, 40). Mill's language continually suggests that he felt coerced by his father; and that he profoundly, although subconsciously, resented his parent's bullying interference. On two occa-

sions Mill permits himself directly to state that his childhood was
dominated by feelings of anxiety and injury. He twice confesses that,
if he felt "always loyally devoted" (*Autobiography*, 32) to James, he
never could fully love, trust, or honor him. "It was," Mill writes,
"one of the most unfavourable of the moral agencies which acted
upon me in my boyhood, that mine was not an education of love
but of fear" (*Early Draft*, 66). "I . . . grew up," he later declares,
"in the absence of love & in the presence of fear: & many & indelible
are the effects of this bringing-up, in the stunting of my moral
growth" (*Early Draft*, 184).

Mill makes it clear in the *Autobiography* that he did not think he
could afford consciously to acknowledge the frustration and the fury
that his situation caused him unconsciously to feel.[7] Throughout his
childhood and youth he seems to have feared that, should he ever
openly resent or actively dissociate himself from his father, he must
forfeit all the "rare" and seemingly indispensable attention that
James had lavished upon him. Even if Mill had been willing to risk
this terrible loss, he did not believe that he possessed enough primary imaginative material to liberate himself from his father's over-
mastering control. He repeatedly suggests in the *Autobiography* that
his entire conception of meaning, value, history, happiness, and love
had been supplied to him by his progenitor. Everything that he experienced and knew evidently had been filtered to him through the
lens of his father's perceptions and opinions. Mill had been allowed
to develop, it appears, no independent or purely personal thoughts,
ideas, or tastes. He had been permitted to establish no societal identifications or institutional affiliations. He had been forbidden to develop avocations or hobbies. He even had been forbidden to find
playmates or to create friendships. In a very disquieting passage,
Mill recalls:

> [My father] carefully kept me from having any great amount
> of intercourse with other boys. He was earnestly bent upon
> my escaping not only the ordinary corrupting influence
> which boys exercise upon boys, but the contagion of vulgar
> modes of thought and feeling. . . . As I had no boy compan-
> ions, and the animal need of physical activity was satisfied by
> walking, my amusements, which were mostly solitary, were
> in general, of a quiet, if not a bookish turn, and gave little

stimulus to any other kind even of mental activity than that
which was already called forth by my studies. (*Autobiography*,
22–23)

Not only did James deny his son "companions" and "amusements."
He as well prohibited him from acquiring "the sentiment of a larger
and freer existence" (*Autobiography*, 35). "I was brought up from the
first," Mill reports, "without any religious belief, in the ordinary
sense of the term" (*Autobiography*, 25). He goes on to declare:

[My father] impressed upon me from the first, that the manner in which the world came into existence was a subject on
which nothing was known. . . . I am thus one of the very
few examples, in this country, of one who has, not thrown off
religious belief, but never had it: I grew up in a negative
state with regard to it. (*Autobiography*, 27–28)

James required his "pupil," it seems, to disbelieve even in pleasure—to disbelieve in strong feelings of any kind. In another of the
Autobiography's extremely unsettling passages, Mill observes:

[My father] had . . . scarcely any belief in pleasure. . . . He
was not insensible to pleasures; but he deemed very few of
them worth the price which, at least in the present state of
society, must be paid for them. . . . His inculcations of
[sobriety] fill a large place in my childhood remembrances.
He thought human life a poor thing at best. . . . For passionate emotions of all sorts, and for everything which has
been said or written in exaltation of them, he professed the
greatest contempt. He regarded them as a form of madness.
'The intense' was with him a bye-word of scornful disap-
probation. He regarded as an aberration of the moral standard
of modern times, compared with that of the ancients, the
great stress laid upon feeling. (*Autobiography*, 30–31)

Adam and Eve at least possessed one another, the serpent, and the
garden as sources of information and as models of alternatives. Mill's
entire experience of existence was bounded by his father's imaginative and philosophical systems. He could no more become free of his

parent than a character in a fiction can become free of his author. Mill subliminally comprehended that his father's "labour, care, and perseverance" were perverse and destructive. But this was not a usable perception, for his father's "care" was all that he had with which to work. Because James's love was irreplaceable, it had to be made to seem irreproachable. Segregated from other people, from God, from nature, and from his own sensibility, Mill had no choice but to force himself consciously to feel "always loyally devoted" to the parent whom he unconsciously realized he should not and could not love. From his severely isolated and parochial point of view, to experience hostility toward his father should be to experience hostility toward himself and hostility toward the condition of being alive. To repudiate James should be to become loveless, nameless, and homeless. To strike out for himself should be to become propelled by a yearning for autonomy into the terrors and the perils of absolute aloneness.

Neither indignation nor unhappiness was includable in Mill's repertoire of allowed emotions. We have seen, however, that he unconsciously did feel bewildered, intimidated, and outraged by James's abusive "method of teaching." Mill could not legitimize—he could not even consciously acknowledge—the displeasure and the disaffection his father made him feel. Neither, though, could he quash these inevitable and appropriate reactions. Throughout his childhood Mill could discover no other alternative but to tolerate an intolerably confusing awareness of double bind. He had to participate in and to value a way of life that he also had to apprehend and to loathe. He felt forced to experience gratitude and "loyalty" toward a parent whom he also felt forced to dread and to despise. His situation may be described in another way. In order to love his father and in order to accept the world that his father offered him, Mill had to deny himself.

Mill's inability ever to articulate or ever to seek reassurance about his impossibly conflicted state of mind greatly exacerbated his predicament. Throughout his childhood he had neither confederates nor confessors. There was no one in his life but his father in whom he might confide. Obviously, though, from his father more than from any other person Mill believed that he must conceal his feelings of distress and discontent. He recalls: "I had no one to whom I desired to express everything which I felt: & the only person I was in communication with, to whom I looked up, I had too much fear of, to make the communication to him of any act or feeling ever a matter of frank impulse or spontaneous inclination" (*Early Draft*, 184).

Mill's ambivalences and tensions were chronic and incapacitating. But he could neither recognize nor reduce them. The nature of his circumstances allowed him no alternative but to ignore his confusions and pains. It became the principal lesson of his sonship that he must sublimate his anxieties and angers; that, indeed, he must anesthetize and internalize his "passionate emotions of all sorts." The *Autobiography* never is more moving or more saddening than in its descriptions of Mill's lifelong effort to deny and to displace the rage that he believed he must not feel toward the all-powerful parent whom he believed he must love.

To this point I have spoken of John as though he were the son solely of James Mill. Of course he was as well the son of James Mill's wife. The *Autobiography* makes us realize that Mill's relationship with his mother was as complicated and as damaging as his relationship with his father. But the principle of complexity and of damage was diametrically different. Harriet Mill seems to have been excessively detached from her child. She seems to have been as underactive in her parenting as James was overly active.

Harriet's inattention and disregard do not appear to have been a completely free choice on her part. To some extent she evidently could not help but seem indifferent to and neglectful of her son. Every contemporary account of the Mills' household describes a severely strained family environment in which Harriet was publicly invalidated as a woman, a wife, and a mother. One observer, Henry Solly, comments:

> [James Mill's] manner to me and other visitors was usually stately, simple, and courteous, and not unkind to his children, though he seemed to take little notice of them except of John; but accustomed as I was to my father's behaviour to my mother, and that of other gentlemen whom I had observed in similar relations, I could not help being rather pained in his manner occasionally to Mrs. Mill. She was a tall

handsome lady, sweet-tempered, with pleasant manners, fond of her children; but I think not much interested in what the elder ones and their father talked about.[8]

Harriet Grote reports that James had married "a stupid woman, 'a housemaide of a woman,' & left off caring for her; [he] treated her as his sqah [*sic*] but was always faithful to her."[9] One of the Mills' daughters gives a more sympathetic but equally harrowing description. She writes:

> My poor mother's married life must have been a frightfully
> hard one, from first to last. . . . Here was an instance of two
> persons, a husband and a wife, living as far apart under the
> same roof, as the north pole from the south; from no fault of
> my poor mother, certainly; but how was a woman with a
> growing family and very small means . . . to be anything
> but a German Hausfrau? How could she "intellectually" be-
> come a companion for such a mind as my father?[10]

As we shall see, Mill himself wrote almost nothing about his mother. What little he did write is shocking in its contempt and in its anger.[11] The infrequency and the brusqueness of his remarks about his mother, the curt and hurt tone of his very few comments, testify to the great impoverishment and painfulness of his relationship with Harriet. Mill does not hesitate to explain why he found it impossible to express either respect or fondness for his mother. He considered her, he tells us, woefully deficient in "personal affection." He declares:

> That rarity in England, a truly warm hearted mother, would
> in the first place have made my father a totally different
> being, and in the second would have made the children grow
> up loving and being loved. But my mother with the very
> best intentions, only knew how to pass her life in drudging
> for them. Whatever she could do for them she did, and they
> liked her, because she was kind to them, but to make herself
> loved, looked up to, or even obeyed, required qualities which
> she unfortunately did not possess. (*Early Draft,* 184)

"Things would have been very different," Mill concludes, if he and his father had been able to live "under the influence of a mother of steady good sense" (*Early Draft*, 184n.).

Repudiated and mocked by her husband, misunderstood and mistrusted by her son, Harriet seems to have received nothing but disdain from the important males in her life. What little we know about her suggests that at some level she acquiesced in and perhaps even enjoyed her disesteem. She luxuriated in her abasement at least to the extent that she accepted it. We do not know of a single instance in which this nullified woman ever attempted to expand the miniscule authority her husband bestowed upon her. Nor are we able to suppose that she made very ample use of the few powers and privileges that James allowed her. John's abrasive and grieving remarks make it clear that Harriet did not often claim even the most primitive perquisite of her maternity: she seems rarely, if ever, to have caressed, bantered with, or even addressed her extraordinarily needy child.

The issue here is not whether Harriet actually felt indifference toward her son. The point is that her son experienced her as being indifferent. He believed that his mother did not love or even care about him. We probably cannot imagine how greatly Harriet's apparent abdication of her maternity disturbed and disordered Mill's development. Psychoanalytic psychology has demonstrated that the quantity and the quality of "personal affection" that a mother gives her child may decisively affect the child's ability to construct a healthy sensory capability. Physical mothering not only feels good to an infant. It also teaches an infant how to identify his own frontiers, and how to recognize those that demarcate other people and the world. As the mother coddles and comforts her child, she shows him that both he and she possess definitive and persisting boundaries. As he accepts his mother's caresses, the infant discovers that he, his parent, and all other persons are discrete and durable, touchable entities. Equally important, the infant discovers that interactions between himself and other selves are possible, expected, and intensely pleasurable. As the mother soothes and settles her child, she helps him comprehend that everything that is not himself may be gentle and hospitable despite its foreignness. Her voice and her hands, which confer definition, acceptance, protection, and pleasure, en-

courage the infant to believe that other people and life itself are loving, welcoming, and highly gratifying. This belief may organize itself into a formal expectation as the child shapes his psychology and
confronts his experience.

The mother's caresses and endearments further teach the child that
feeling pleasure is one of his most important functions. As he feels
himself being manually and verbally stimulated, the infant gradually discerns that he *is* what is being pleasured. Equally significant,
he discovers that his ability to experience and to express pleasure
delights the parent who is the source of his excitement. The child
quickly perceives that he may expand this principle into a system of
projection and power. Mothering pleases him. He communicates his
pleasure. His mother rewards his communications with renewed
and protracted, progressively more fervent hugs, kisses, and mur-
murings. These gratifications, which continue the original gratifications' work of defining, validating, and reinforcing the infant's nas-
cent ego activity, feel particularly pleasurable to him because he has
sought and, so to speak, willed or even created the phenomena. As
the sequence of these solicitations and compensations occurs and re-
.occurs, the infant learns that it is his own willingness to feel pleasure that inspires affection and precipitates contentment. He concludes that he is given affection because his mother and, potentially,
all other people find him lovable in his power to ask for and to respond to love.

In time the successfully mothered child allows these initially tentative intuitions to operate as an unconscious ontology. He subrationally assumes that his personal substance is discriminable from
that of the world, and from that of all other people. He trusts that
his worth is inherent: he believes that he normally may expect other
persons to acknowledge, to love, and to satisfy him. Perhaps most
important, he concludes that the mechanism by which he most sat-
isfactorily can proclaim his discreteness and induce his pleasure is
the activity of communicating. The act of expressing, and particularly the act of exchanging language, proposes itself to him as the
natural means by which a person may define and fulfill his fundamental imaginative requirements. Upon these perceptions and identifications the successfully nurtured child confidently relies. His preludial, organizational assumptions establish themselves as a reservoir

of certitude and hope upon which he continually may draw as he enters into his relation with nature, history, other people, and himself.[12]

From infancy through latency, from latency to adulthood, Mill was deprived of this fundamental psychological heritage. In the place of his effectively nonexistent mother stood an overwhelmingly extant father. As we have seen, it was not a part of James's programme to mother his child. Instead of endearments and caresses, he supplied his child with injunctions, perorations, and reproofs. Instead of spontaneity and openness, he offered his child rituals, routines, and repressions. The discourse of John's familism was wholly intellective and almost completely humiliating. He always was made to understand that he possessed neither singularity nor, in his own right, dignity and worth. "Whatever I knew more than others," Mill continually was told, "could not be ascribed to any merit in me, but to the very unusual advantage which had fallen to my lot, of having a father who was able to teach me, and willing to give the necessary trouble and time; [I was told] that it was no matter of praise to me, if I knew more than those who had not a similar advantage, but the deepest disgrace to me if I did not" (*Autobiography*, 22).

Throughout his childhood and youth, Mill learned almost nothing about the mechanics or the uses of pleasurable emotion. He was taught that human beings are predominantly rational rather than sensual creatures. He was made to think that the universe is purely phrenic, and that he must invent a purely phrenic, entirely impersonal way of moving through it. Prohibited virtually all subliminal experience, Mill was forced to believe in and to inhabit an almost totally supraliminal, almost constantly chastising world.

As bewildering and as damaging to Mill as his parents' lack of "personal affection" was the complex and perverse psychosexual configuration that inhered in his family. Although his parents lived "as far apart under the same roof, as the north pole from the south," they seem to have cleaved together in their symbiotic dependence upon one another's dysfunctions. James, we have observed, needed to master. Harriet needed to be mastered. Connected by their oppositeness, the Mills apparently preserved their strained marriage by treating their eldest child as the site upon which they could act out the dynamics of their separate diseases. The *Autobiography* indicates that James expressed the completeness of his need for supremacy by completely dominating John. Harriet expressed the completeness of her need for insignificance by becoming completely dominated by John. The son occupied a position of extraordinary centrality in the polity of his family because he consented to serve as the symbolization and the object of his parents' most urgently felt ideas about themselves. In effect he became the vessel of his parents' intercourse. James and Harriet sustained a conjugal response to one another, it seems, by making a disparate but related, figuratively connubial response to John.[13]

The *Autobiography's* anxious and sorrowing account of the Mills' relationship makes it apparent that for each of the family's members—but particularly for John—this state of affairs became extremely problematic. The specific nature of John's situation may perhaps best be understood in terms provided by psychoanalytic theory. Psychoanalysts have discovered that in the course of his psychosexual evolution every male child develops a complicated set of instincts and emotions that he directs toward his parents, but that actually refers to and expresses one of his earliest and most significant responses to himself. Freud describes the phenomenon in this way:

> When a boy (from the age of two or three) has entered the phallic phase of his libidinal development . . . he becomes his mother's lover. He wishes to possess her physically in such ways as he has divined from his observations and intuitions about sexual life, and he tries to seduce her by showing her the male organ which he is proud to own. In a word, his early awakened masculinity seeks to take his father's place with her; his father has hitherto in any case been an envied model to the boy, owing to the physical strength which he perceives in him and the authority with which he finds him clothed. His father now becomes a rival who stands in his way and whom he would like to get rid of. . . . This is the subject of the Oedipus complex. . . . Under the conditions of our civilization it is invariably doomed to a frightening end.[14]

The "frightening end" to which Freud refers is the successful but psychologically devastating resolution of the Oedipus complex.

Freud believed that "under the conditions of our civilization" the male child gradually discovers that he must redefine his instinctive response to his mother and to his father. His parents and the culture in which he lives together compel the child to transform his erotic response to his mother into a merely affectionate relation. The son who had been an aspiring lover gradually feels impelled to convert his instinctive erogenous excitement into merely filial love and its abstract, imperfectly satisfying forms of demonstrativeness. The child simultaneously finds it necessary to alter his anxious reaction to his father into a formal identification with his father's prowess. The child is taught to interpret his subconscious trepidation and resentment as conscious respect and love. He learns to channel his fearful and furious sense of competition with his father into ambition, hard work, or some other mode of socially agreeable aggressiveness. His parents and the civilization in which he has his being require the child drastically to inhibit his most authentic and his most compelling desires. The child becomes forced to realize that he can function in his family and operate in the world only by radically censoring his elemental humanity.[15]

Freud believed that the Oedipus complex is experienced by all persons. Mill's Oedipal instinctions, however, seem to have been peculiarly strong—and peculiarly inverted. From his earliest infancy Mill was taught that his mother was inept, vapid, vulgar, and remote; and that his father was capable, creative, wise, and affectionate. Throughout his childhood Mill was directed to desire and idolize his father and to distrust, resent, and envy his mother. To all "things which my father told me," he comments, "I gave implicit credence" (*Autobiography*, 22). For his mother's ideas and opinions, he reports, "I never had the slightest regard" (*Early Draft*, 56n.). Toward his father, Mill repeatedly suggests, he felt a vast and unquestioning devotion. He obsessively detested his mother. Psychoanalysis recognizes as an abnormal syndrome the inverse Oedipal identification that Mill seems to have developed. In those instances when the Oedipal love-object becomes reversed—when, as in the case of Mill, longing for the father and aversion to the mother prevail—a male child is said to demonstrate a "negative" or an "inverted Oedipus complex."[16] Whether or not Mill's Oedipal instincts were clinically "negative," he unquestionably felt forced by the circumstances of his life to undervalue his mother and to overvalue his father.

Not only did Mill's early experience lead him to invert his Oedipal neurosis. Everything we know about his childhood indicates that his Oedipal neurosis was never conclusively interdicted. Although he was not permitted literally to accomplish or even consciously to define the full programme of his "negative" syndrome, his parents did allow Mill subconsiously to feel and symbolically to act out the syndrome's principal identifications and impulses. The *Autobiography* suggests that day after day the Mills teased and titillated their son by seeming to participate in his impossible conception of the family. Each morning James consigned Harriet to the kitchen and welcomed John to his study. Each afternoon James fled from his "sqah" so that he might walk and talk with his favored child. In company James shunned his "German Hausfrau" and triumphantly brought forward his little boy. Within the circle of the family he invited John to share his labors and to enter into his most intimate reflections. Harriet, too, participated in this inadvertent teasing. She silently consented to John's appropriation of her functions and roles. She behaved as though her child's way of reconstructing the family suited and excited herself. No matter how often or how thoroughly he ultimately became frustrated, Mill could not help but continually exult in his parents' nearly complete fulfillment of the subrational fantasies that shaped his imagination. Everything in his daily life conspired to suggest that one day he might unequivocally dispose of his feared and hated mother, and unequivocally attract to himself his all-powerful and longed-for father. John Mill may be regarded, I believe, as one of the very few children who ever has lived "under the conditions of our civilization" who has been *encouraged* to develop and to explore the Oedipal pathology.

Mill's family achieved great internal strength because of its power to organize and to fulfill the intrapsychical demands of each of its members. The Mills fused to one another because they created together a centripetal circle of "inverted" knowledge and "negative" love. This is not to suggest that John's experience of family gave him comfort and happiness. No matter how fully his parents subconsciously welcomed their son's Oedipal yearnings and maneuvers, they never allowed him decisively to satisfy his imagination's complex and compelling requirements. By day John could displace Harriet and symbolically wed himself to James. But James continued to pass his nights with his seemingly usurped spouse; and with her he begat child after child. John could not fail to recognize in the persons of his numerous siblings an absolute demonstration of the fact that his Oedipal design was constitutionally incomplete. [17] In the end, he was forced to acknowledge, it was marriage and sex with the wife rather than colloquy with the son that the father definitively preferred.

Mill's situation could not have been more confusing or more wounding. To the extent that he successfully could constitute himself as the fulfillment of his father's conceits, he could perpetuate his father's regard and comply with the demands of his own psychology. Yet Mill never could settle into gratification and security. His deepest libidinal drives were tantalizingly fostered but never satisfied. Despite its impressive approximation of total psychosexual compensation, Mill's early experience was bewildering and mutilating in its terrible mixture of compulsive stimulation and chronic, unmitigable frustration.

Earlier I remarked that Mill could not afford to acknowledge how anxious and how angry his experiences made him feel. I did not intend to suggest that Mill failed to react to his experience. He reacted intensely; but he required himself to react subconsciously. As we read the *Autobiography*, we discover some of the mechanisms of Mill's subconscious reactions and some of the costs which those mechanisms entailed.

We discover, for example, that Mill did not allow himself to develop elementary behavioral skills at an ordinary rate or pace. The most visible of what he calls "the very considerable drawbacks" (*Early Draft*, 54n.) produced by his exigent situation was the apparently quite serious retardation of his speech and motor-skill functions. "I was far longer than children generally are," he reports, "before I could put on my clothes. I know not how many years passed before I could tie a knot. My articulation was long imperfect; one letter *r*, I could not pronounce until I was nearly sixteen. I never could, nor can I now, do anything requiring the smallest manual dexterity" (*Early Draft*, 178–79). Each of these abilities—the ability to pronounce strong consonants, the ability to clothe oneself, the ability to be competent—draws upon and expresses one's consciousness of being a discrete and an integrated person. By electing to speak and to perform ineptly, Mill seems to have been declaring that he did not regard himself as a coherent and a capable organism. By refusing to become skilled, he seems to have been communicating his confusion about how to be human.

He seems also to have been communicating resentment and exacting revenge. We have learned that Mill had many reasons to feel anger. But he had singularly few opportunities to express and to relieve anger. It appears to have been in order to voice his rage against his father, and perhaps even in order to avenge himself upon his father, that Mill chose to mature so slowly. James was abundantly talented and extraordinarily decisive. It seems likely that John subconsciously decided to become rudimentarily untalented and indecisive because he wanted to frustrate and to humiliate the remarkably capable parent who had frustrated and humiliated him.[18]

This mingling of confusion and ineptitude with rage, this willingness to inflict damage upon himself in response to the damage that had been inflicted upon him, became Mill's fundamental way of coping with his experience. Throughout his life he tried to control his debilitating anxieties by regarding his father as a hero, his mother as a nonentity, and himself as a radically flawed, almost helplessly incompetent overachiever. Early in the *Autobiography*, for example, he declares: "In all . . . natural gifts, I am rather below than above par" (*Autobiography*, 19–20). "I grew up," he reports, "with great inaptness in the common affairs of every day life" (*Early Draft*, 178). This "inaptness," he insists, "was not owing to the mode of my education but to a certain natural slowness & to a certain mental and moral indolence which, but for the immense amount of mental cultivation which my father gave me, would probably have prevented me from either being or doing anything worthy of note" (*Early Draft*, 182). There evidently was no limit to Mill's impulse to disparage himself and to exalt his father. At one point he goes so far as to declare:

> I was, as my father continually told me, like a person who had not the organs of sense. . . . My father was the extreme opposite. . . . His senses & his mental faculties were always on the alert; he carried decision & energy of character in his whole manner & into every action of his life: & this, as much as his talents, contributed to the great impression which he

always made upon those with whom he came in personal contact. (*Early Draft*, 179)

"What I could do," Mill concludes, "assuredly could be done by any boy or girl of average capacity and healthy physical constitution; and if I have accomplished anything, I owe it, among other fortunate circumstances, to the fact that through the early training bestowed on me by my father, I started, I may fairly say, with an advantage of a quarter of a century over my contemporaries" (*Autobiography*, 20).

We cannot fail to notice that in each of these passages the nominative sense almost is not available to Mill. He scarcely can define or even refer to his own consciousness and achievements. Whenever Mill does find it possible directly to speak of himself, his language indicates that he can conceive of his character solely as an inadequacy or as an absence. What "I" discretely am, he continually remarks, is a compound of "inaptness" and "indolence." What "I" have done, he repeatedly observes, is totally attributable to the "fortunate" presence of James. It appears to have been one of the major "drawbacks" of his childhood that Mill could conceive of and accept his own sensibility only by denigrating himself and celebrating his sire. He seems to have emerged from his early experience with an inability to like, to trust, or to assert himself; and with a need to locate what little identity and confidence he could claim in his power to aggrandize and to associate himself with his father.

As we read passages of the sort which I have cited, we become aware of another peculiar circumstance. I have observed that Mill's recognitions of himself almost always occurred as expressions of contempt for his deficiencies and failures. He invariably regarded himself, I have suggested, as a vast inadequacy. He defined himself as a strange, stunted nonentity barely capable of consciousness and activity. We should expect that a man who developed such a hostile attitude toward his own character must write about himself sadly, or shamefully, or at least solemnly. But Mill's comments about himself sound tranquil and pleased. His language is oddly serene, as if he liked defaming himself. We cannot definitively determine why it gratified Mill to write about himself in a manner which should have made most other persons feel humiliated and horrified. We can speculate, though, that he felt satisfied with his abusive way of regarding himself because he found it both logical and calming.

Earlier I remarked that Mill's parents gravely inhibited his ability to identify and to enjoy himself. His mother and father did not permit him, I suggested, either imaginatively or libidinally to discern his own reality and to believe in his own worth. Mill seems to have dealt with this tragic and scarring deprivation by trying to make his parents' perceptions his own. He appears to have solved the great puzzle of his own feelings of rejection and emptiness by fictionalizing or reinterpreting his experience. In effect he seems to have decided: I am nothing. My mother is nothing. My father is everything. My mother could only exist, and I could only exist, as pale reflections of my father. My mother recognized this. She abandoned me, and she deferred absolutely to my father. She seemed unloving. Really, though, she was caring for me by giving me over to my father's protection and care. She wanted me to be greater than myself. My father wanted this, too. His parenting seemed despotic and confining. But it was loving of him to tyrannize me. He had to master and to rule me, because he realized that I needed to be shaped, guided, and made functional. Initially I believed that my mother's desertion and my father's despotism were brutal behaviors. Now I realize that these were tender acts; for my parents perceived my lack of substance, and they decided to deed to me a part of my father's substance. Had I been raised in any other, more ordinary way, I should have become *totally* "below par," wholly "inapt," utterly "unworthy" and inconsequential. Once I had feared that my parents hated me. Now I know that in truth they loved me.

The intensely self-deprecating tone that characterizes Mill's descriptions of himself probably was unconsciously deliberate. By impugning his own abilities and accomplishments, Mill explained the devastating riddle of his parents' attitudes and actions. Equally important, he discovered a way to convert his crippling anger and grief into emotions that felt to him like those of acceptance and gratitude. It is for this reason, I believe, that Mill's reminiscences sound so confident and pleased when he is advancing extremely self-destructive judgments and views. Ultimately Mill served himself by demeaning himself. By undervaluing himself and overvaluing his father, he created a means by which to transform his mystifying and devitalizing history into a coherent and somewhat agreeable mythology.

Mill's unconscious strategy of interiorizing and displacing his chronic conflicts and confusions was successful, in the sense that he managed to conceal his "passionate emotions" from his father and from himself. It is important to recognize, however, that Mill could not organize his system of reverse or negative egotism into a full identification. He could not manipulate his subrational idea of his own inferiority and his father's godhood into a principle of positive self-knowledge. The only kind of personal awareness that Mill could develop was that of unawareness. He could know himself only by knowing his inadequacies. This was a type of consciousness, but it could not evolve into a consciousness of strong and active selfhood.

Mill seems to have comprehended this fact. To Carlyle he once wrote: "I have an unshakeable faith in others though not in myself." [19] He confirms and extends this view of himself in the *Autobiography*. In a memorable and frightening passage, he declares:

> I was not at all aware that my attainments were anything unusual at my age. If I accidentally had my attention drawn to the fact that some other boy knew less than myself—which happened less often than might be imagined—I concluded not that I knew much, but that he, for some reason or other, knew little, or that his knowledge was of a different kind from mine. My state of mind was not humility, but neither was it arrogance. I never thought of saying to myself, I am, or I can do, so and so. I neither estimated myself highly or lowly: I did not estimate myself at all. (*Autobiography*, 21)

These remarks do not indicate that Mill suffered from apatheia or accidie. Throughout the *Autobiography* Mill makes it clear that he could receive stimuli and experience emotion. He also makes it clear, however, that he could not sense and behave as an organized personality. He acted and reacted, it seems, as a new and distinctly modern kind of man. In the first thoroughly industrialized civilization, John Mill developed a thoroughly industrialized imagination. As though he were a power loom or a steam jenny, he produced almost completely impersonal perceptions and associations. He could sense and he could function. But he sensed and functioned in ways that had little to do with the structures and the purposes of fully characterized intelligence. Mill stood a fair chance of becoming, as he himself suggested, "a mere reasoning machine" (*Autobiography*, 66). His manner of reacting to his experience caused him to seem, as Carlyle less discreetly put the matter, "a 'made' or manufactured man, having had a certain impress of opinion stamped on [him] which [he] could only reproduce" (*Autobiography*, 93).

A particularly unfortunate consequence of his failure to become an integrated person was the fact that Mill developed severe limitations in his power to desire, to express, and to act. Mill knew this. He understood that the most "baneful" effect of his subconsciously deliberate self-suppression was "the stunting of [his] moral growth." In an early version of the *Autobiography*, he wrote:

> Without knowing or believing that I was reserved, I grew up
> with an instinct of closeness. I had no one to whom I desired
> to express everything which I felt. . . . My circumstances
> tended to form a character, close & reserved from habit &
> want of impulse. (*Early Draft*, 183, 184)

This "stunting" seemed to Mill to have produced two discrete but related results. On the one hand, he thought, he could not consciously love "with any warmth of affection" (*Early Draft*, 183). Nor, he feared, could he consciously wish, intend, or will. Mill describes his emotional "backwardness" in a striking and sad passage. He writes:

> To have been, through childhood, under the constant rule of
> a strong will, certainly is not favourable to strength of will. I
> was so much accustomed to expect to be told what to
> do . . . that I acquired a habit of leaving my responsibility as
> a moral agent to rest on my father, my conscience never
> speaking to me except by his voice. The things *not* to do were
> mostly provided for by his precepts, rigidly enforced when-
> ever violated, but the things which I *ought* to do I hardly ever
> did of my own mere motion, but waited till he told me to do
> them. . . . I thus acquired a habit of backwardness, of wait-
> ing to follow the lead of others, an absence of moral spon-
> taneity, an inactivity of the moral sense & even to a large
> extent, of the intellect, unless roused by the appeal of some
> one else. (*Early Draft*, 185)

We cannot know if this was literally true. The important circumstance is that Mill believed it was true. He believed that he experienced almost nothing from within. He believed that he could identify in himself almost no purely personal "conscience," "motion," "moral sense," or "intellect." His impulses felt to him like a host of implants that had been grafted onto him by his father. His desires and his inclinations seemed to himself involuntary and unauthentic, "inactive" and "backward."

The primary "drawback" of Mill's childhood was the fact that his entire psychology developed inversely and incompletely. In order to give "voice," "spontaneity," and "sense" to himself, he found it necessary to create and to submit to an external "agent" who could seem to him more organic, more valid, and more valuable than himself. In order to identify "strength," "will," and genuineness in his own character, he felt impelled to idolize and to enslave himself to an all-powerful, highly remote, and thoroughly intimidating "some one else."

Mill gradually extended his excessively filial way of organizing his intelligence. In the *Autobiography* he indicates that he eventually came to regard not his father alone but a number of other authoritative male authors as his "moral agent" and his "consciousness." Jeremy Bentham seemed especially appealing and useful to him. Mill's description of his initial reaction to Bentham makes it evident that he believed he had found in his father's colleague and closest friend much more than merely a stimulating teacher. He remarks:

> When I laid down the last volume of the Traité I had become
> a different being. The 'principle of utility' understood as
> Bentham had understood it, and applied in the manner in
> which he applied it through these three volumes, fell exactly
> into its place as the keystone which held together the de-
> tached and fragmentary component parts of my knowledge
> and beliefs. It gave unity to my conception of things. I now
> had opinions; a creed, a doctrine, a philosophy; in one among
> the best senses of the word, a religion; the inculcation and
> diffusion of which could be made the principal outward pur-
> pose of a life. . . . The vista of improvement which he did
> open was sufficiently large and brilliant to light up my life,

as well as to give a definite shape to my aspirations. (*Autobi-ography*, 42–43)

These are excited word choices. But they also are deliberate and precise usages. The paragraph suggests that Bentham's "Traité" conferred upon Mill not simply a structure and a system for his thought, but as well an identification in the full psychoanalytic sense of the word. The "three volumes" affected him, it appears, as though they were a wonderfully organized and coherent version of himself. In Bentham's book Mill discovered, he believed, a means by which he might understand and unify his own personality's "detached and fragmentary component parts." Working from this "turning point in [his] mental history" (*Autobiography*, 41), Mill apparently felt it possible to integrate and to inspirit his entire character. He reports that he gradually became able to fashion for himself everything that his father's pedagogy had failed to supply: "a unity," "a creed," "an outward purpose," "a definite shape," a "large and brilliant" feeling of hopefulness, determination, and energy.

As with Bentham, so with Locke, Hume, Hartley, Berkeley, Reid, Stewart, Brown, and Grote. Mill suggests in the *Autobiography* that by 1821 he derived almost all his conscious emotions and "aspirations" from his reading. He reacted to texts as most other men react to living persons and to historical phenomena. By seizing upon and interiorizing other writers' ideas and feelings, Mill seems for a time to have succeeded in fashioning that consciousness of coherence, engagement, and pleasure which more normally constituted people achieve from more direct encounters with experience.

It is significant that the terms of this identification seemed to Mill to be completely impersonal. In the *Autobiography* he is careful to describe the sense of enterprise or mission that he received from Bentham as an "*outward* purpose." He is careful to speak of the existence that he believed Bentham offered him as "*a* life." His excitement appears to have been generated by the possibility of achieving unity and order. And unity and order seem to have presented themselves to him as dividends of selflessness or neuterdom.

We are in a position to understand why this may have been so. We have discovered that Mill's consciousness was chronically conflicted: he continually felt angry at the parent whom he believed he needed to adore. We have learned that Mill tried to cure his tensions and confusions by deconstructing himself and idealizing his father. His way of responding to literature appears to have developed this principle to a highly gratifying extreme. Mill did not simply read a book. He seems to have believed that he could cause himself to flee into an author's consciousness. He seems to have imagined that everything that was himself—everything furious and loving, everything pained and yearning, everything "detached and fragmentary"— could be made to assume the beautiful integrity, solidness, resolution, value, and majesty of a masterful text.

An important element in this fantasy's appeal for Mill probably was the fact that his attitudes about his uses of literature thoroughly harmonized with his father's. James, too, apparently possessed little ability to distinguish between literature and life. James, too, supposed that texts and sensibilities were cooperative and even consubstantial. The son's overdetermined manner of reading allowed him to liberate himself from his parent by introducing him to new kinds of imagination and knowledge. Crucially, however, John could feel while he was reading that he was acting and reacting as his father would wish him to do. The achievement which was contained in this complicated fantasy was considerable—and considerably inventive. In his attitude toward reading, particularly in his attitude toward reading the works of his father's close friend, Mill found a way to individuate himself without consciously challenging the supremacy of his parent; and without consciously challenging the sovereignty of his hysterical response to his parent. By reading in his highly excited way, Mill created a means by which to perpetuate his Oedipal pathology while persuading himself that he had learned to avoid and perhaps even to cure it.

Mill entered his majority conceiving of books and of authors as "the keystone" that defined and animated his existence. He soon "began to carry on [his] intellectual cultivation by writing still more than by reading." During the summer of 1822, he wrote his "first argumentative essay" (*Autobiography*, 45). Between 1822 and 1826 he produced numerous works of what he described in the *Autobiography* as "youthful propagandism" on behalf of his father's loosely organized but "rapidly rising" (*Autobiography*, 54, 60) political party.

Helping to shape "the movement of opinion among the most

cultivated part of the new generation" (*Autobiography*, 71) for some time stirred and satisfied Mill. In the *Autobiography* he recalls the years of his apprenticeship as a period of seemingly uncomplicated dedication and delight. He remarks:

> I had what might truly be called an object in life; to be a reformer of the world. My conception of my own happiness was entirely identified with this object. . . . As a serious and permanent personal satisfaction to rest upon, my whole reliance was placed on this: and I was accustomed to felicitate myself on the certainty of a happy life which I enjoyed, through placing my happiness in something durable and distant, in which some progress might be always making, while it could never be exhausted by complete attainment. . . . The general improvement going on in the world and the idea of myself as engaged with others in struggling to promote it, seemed enough to fill up an interesting and animated existence. (*Autobiography*, 80)

Here, as so often, Mill's uses of language reveal a great deal about the origins and the meanings of his subconscious thought. We have observed that Mill's early experience forced him to doubt his actuality and his worth. We also have seen that throughout his youth Mill yearned to unite himself psychically and perhaps even physically with his omnipotent father. The passage at hand suggests that writing his "youthful propagandism" allowed Mill symbolically to fulfill this programme. As he wrote his first essay, he evidently could feel that he at last had "entirely identified" himself "with [an] object—an "object" which was "durable and distant" and altogether discriminable from his own problematic and objectionable, uncomfortably libidinal self. Insofar as Mill was able to regard himself as a discrete person, he apparently conceived of himself as a highly disciplined disciple who loved and worked in absolute association with "others": with Bentham and the younger Utilitarians, but also, far more significantly, with his father. Authoring echoic versions of James's "very decided political and philosophical opinions" (*Autobiography*, 62) apparently seemed to Mill a way of satisfying his subliminal hope that he could "rest upon" a "serious and permanent personal" affiliation with his parent's ideas, beliefs, and purposes.

During his early years as a writer he could "felicitate [himself] on the certainty of a happy life" because his activities seemed to be figuratively accomplishing the inverted Oedipal unification for which he always had longed.

At one point in his account of his experience between 1822 and 1826, Mill almost consciously addresses the intimate relationship between the demands of his Oedipus complex and the pleasures of his career and his craft. He comments:

> It was my father's opinions which gave the distinguishing character to the Benthamic or utilitarian propagandism of that time. They fell singly scattered from him in a continued stream principally in three channels. One was through me, the only mind directly formed by his instructions, and through whom considerable influence was exercised over various young men who became, in their turn, propagandists.
> (*Autobiography*, 62–63)

The psychosexual significance of Mill's identifications scarcely could be more explicitly expressed. The passage indicates that the act of writing at least initially attracted and gratified Mill because it confirmed his cherished "idea of [himself]" as his parent's chosen "channel." More specifically, Mill's language makes it apparent that his work allowed him to conceive of himself as his father's symbolic phallus. In the son's essays, the paragraph implicitly declares, the parent's persuasions and passions "flowed . . . in a continued stream." This cooperative or mutual lexical and sexual emission seemed to Mill to have inseminated and engendered a whole family of "young men" who adhered to and who propagated James's politics and policies. Through John's symbolically uxorial work, this is to say, James became able almost universally to expand his paternity.

It is difficult to imagine a more nearly complete Oedipal excitement. In this strikingly acute, although altogether unaware self-analysis, Mill reveals that his project as a writer closely paralleled his project as a son. He became an author, it seems, primarily in order that he might author himself as his parent's preferred and indispensable partner.[20] Mill apparently derived so much pleasure and so much confidence from his early work because his "propagandism" seemed to him both to intensify and to relieve the intricate Oedipal drama that had "animated" and severely confused his imagination.

In this context, it was most important for Mill that his early work as a writer allowed him to feel autonomous and bold at the same moment that he satisfied his lifelong compulsion to live subserviently and selflessly. Between 1822 and 1826, he did little more than to ape his father's opinion and prose styles. But as he composed his mimetic, essentially inert essays, it evidently seemed to Mill that he was creating his own ideas and language. He seems to have derived so much happiness from his first experiences as an author at least in part because in his early essays the imitation to which his education had condemned him succeeded in masking itself as invention. Acquiescence presented itself as independence. Submission proposed itself as evolution. His initial work as a writer seemed to Mill to solve the most debilitating problem of his childhood. In the making of his "youthful propagandism" he had discovered, he believed, an ingenious way to simultaneously incorporate himself with his father and establish the consoling "idea of [himself]" as a liberated adult.

Mill quickly learned that his "idea of [himself]" as a resolved and a resourceful person was delusional. He reports in the *Autobiography* that during the autumn of 1826 his entire "conception of things" abruptly abolished itself. He became afflicted, he recalls, with an agonized cognition of listlessness and despair. Neither activity nor awareness seemed attractive or even plausible to him. He could feel nothing but melancholy and mourning.

Mill's description of his terrible mental and emotional condition has become one of the *Autobiography*'s most celebrated passages. He writes:

> I was in a dull state of nerves, such as everybody is occasionally liable to; unsusceptible to enjoyment or pleasurable excitement; one of those moods when what is pleasure at other times, becomes insipid or indifferent; the state, I should think, in which converts to Methodism usually are, when smitten by their first 'conviction of sin.' In this frame of mind it occurred to me to put the question directly to my-

self, 'Suppose that all your objects in life were realized; that
all the changes in institutions and opinions which you are
looking forward to, could be completely effected at this very
instant: would this be a great joy and happiness to you?' And
an irrepressible self-consciousness distinctly answered, 'No!'
At this my heart sank within me: the whole foundation on
which my life was constructed fell down. All my happiness
was to have been found in the continual pursuit of this end.
The end had ceased to charm, and how could there ever again
be any interest in the means? I seemed to have nothing left to
live for. (*Autobiography*, 81)

Literature written during the nineteenth century in Europe records
many instances of profound and persisting depression. None was
more extreme or more protracted than this. Mill completely lost the
ability to feel. All life seemed to him a "vapid uninteresting thing"
(*Autobiography*, 88). Especially his own existence affected him as
being vacuous and sterile. He recalls:

I was . . . without real desire for the ends which I had been
so carefully fitted for: no delight in virtue or the general
good, but also just as little in anything else. The fountains of
vanity and ambition seemed to have dried up within me, as
completely as those of benevolence. (*Autobiography*, 84)

He could derive comfort from none of his usual pursuits or associates. His father seemed especially unqualified to counsel or to con-
sole him. Mill comments:

In vain I sought relief from my favourite books . . . , from
which I had always hitherto drawn strength and animation. . . . I sought no comfort by speaking to others of what
I felt. If I had loved any one sufficiently to make confiding
my griefs a necessity, I should not have been in the condition
I was. . . . My father, to whom it would have been natural
to me to have recourse in any practical difficulties, was the
last person to whom, in such a case as this, I looked for help.
Everything convinced me that he had no knowledge of any
such mental state as I was suffering from, and that even if he

could be made to understand it, he was not the physician
who could heal it. (*Autobiography*, 81–82)

Mill could not even believe that his "mental malady" (*Autobiography*,
84) was significant or singular. "I felt," he reports, "that mine was
not an interesting or in any way respectable disease. There was
nothing in it to attract sympathy" (*Autobiography*, 81). Estranged
from his entire "fabric of happiness," insupportably "*blasé* and indifferent," racked with loneliness and "dejection," (*Autobiography*, 84,
87), he descended into suicidal despair. In one of the saddest passages in the *Autobiography*, Mill writes: "I frequently asked myself, if
I could, or if I was bound to go on living, when life must be passed
in this manner. I generally answered to myself, that I did not think
I could possibly bear it beyond a year" (*Autobiography*, 85).

Mill believed that his education was responsible for this "crisis in
[his] mental history" (*Autobiography*, 80). It seemed to him that he
never had been taught how to develop "any natural tie" with "the
real connexions between Things." He comments:

> I now saw, or thought I saw, what I had always before re-
> ceived with incredulity—that the habit of analysis has a ten-
> dency to wear away the feelings: as indeed it has when no
> other mental habit is cultivated, and the analysing spirit re-
> mains without its natural complements and correc-
> tions. . . . My education, I thought, had failed to create
> [feelings] in sufficient strength to resist the dissolving influ-
> ence of analysis, while the whole course of my intellectual
> cultivation had made precocious and premature analysis the
> inveterate habit of my mind. (*Autobiography*, 83–84)

The anger that shapes these remarks is indirect but chilling. For the
reasons I have tried to define, Mill could not allow himself consciously to condemn his father. But he could allow himself to condemn his education; and he could allow himself to recognize that
the education which had incapacitated him "was wholly [his father's]
work" (*Autobiography*, 82). As he suffered through the "dry heavy
dejection of the melancholy winter of 1826–1827" (*Autobiography*,
84), Mill for the first time in his life permitted himself to comprehend that his parent's "teachings" had terrified and traumatized him.

Equally important, he permitted himself to realize that his crippling disorders were "beyond the power of [his parent's] remedies" (*Autobiography*, 82).

Mill ultimately found a "remedy" of his own for his "mental malady." The remedy that he found has become almost as famous as the illness from which he recovered. Mill reports that he reconstructed—or that he created—his power to feel by accepting literature as a healing agent. He recalls:

> I was reading, accidentally, Marmontel's *Memoirs,* and came to the passage which relates his father's death, the distressed position of the family, and the sudden inspiration by which he, then a mere boy, felt and made them feel that he would be everything to them—would supply the place of all that they had lost. A vivid conception of the scene and its feelings came over me, and I was moved to tears. From this moment my burthen grew lighter. The oppression of the thought that all feeling was dead in me, was gone. I was no longer hopeless: I was not a stock or a stone. I had still, it seemed, some of the material out of which all worth of character, and all capacity for happiness, are made. . . . The cloud gradually drew off, and I again enjoyed life: and though I had several relapses, some of which lasted many months, I never again was as miserable as I had been. (*Autobiography*, 85)[21]

Rarely before has literature been exploited in so appropriative or in so explicitly therapeutic a manner. Mill seems to have achieved the capacity to feel by internalizing the *Memoirs'* "scenes" and "feelings." He evidently reacted to the text with so much imaginative force that he managed to convert the book's representations of pathos and passion into personal experiences. He did not read, it appears, so much as he co-opted and consumed. Life became once again "vivid," affective, and appealing to him less on its own terms than on terms engineered for him by another man's memories.

We readily can imagine that literature may be made to operate in a consoling or in a restorative way. It is difficult to understand, however, how so unsophisticated a work as Marmontel's *Memoirs* could have appealed to and rehabilitated so sophisticated, and so sophisticatedly distressed, a mind as John Mill's. One of the *Autobiography*'s critics has suggested that Mill responded to the *Memoirs* with so much immediacy and intensity because his manner of reading the book provided him with a means by which to externalize and to control the tensions that had precipitated his illness. Dr. A. W. Levi speculates that Mill's "mental crisis" was provoked by the fact that he subconsciously despised his father and subliminally longed for his father's death. Mill developed his "malady," Dr. Levi contends, because he could not any longer endure the remorse and the fear that accompanied his progressively more conscious patricidal fury. From this point of view, reading the *Memoirs* may have helped Mill relieve his disabling "'conviction of sin'" because it allowed him to exteriorize his unacceptable wrath. Dr. Levi explains:

> In reading Marmontel's account John could in the process of identification and without guilt bring to full consciousness the idea that his father in the natural course of things would some day die, and that he himself would assume the dominating role. . . . In experiencing his father's death and the freedom which this would mean to his own ego, but under the literary and imaginative circumstances which would absolve him of the guilty wishes themselves, [Mill] brought to the surface of consciousness what had hitherto been laboriously repressed, and by this cathartic act spontaneously found the real solution for his mental crisis.[22]

This is a convincing analysis. It seems to me, however, that Dr. Levi underestimates the extremeness of Mill's situation. We have learned that Mill could not afford even *subconsciously* to distrust, to dislike, or to distance himself from the parent who had defined him. He perhaps could question the system of education that had conditioned his life. But he could not repudiate his educator. For his educator had made him believe that he was absolutely without internal resources. No matter how deeply he resented James's manipulating and maiming pedagogy, Mill seems completely to have accepted the delusion that he could not survive without James's guidance, sympathy, support, and sanction. I believe that he could not allow himself even subliminally to desire his father's death because he felt certain that his father was the origin and the core of what little coherence, energy, and value he possessed.

Yet, as we have seen, Mill did fear and hate the father whom he
also loved and needed. He could not abolish his frightened indignation; nor could he permit himself to feel it. The need to hate and the
need not to hate seem to have become equally compelling. However, these antithetical compulsions refused to cohere into a single,
compromised emotion. On the scale that we encounter in the case of
John Mill, anger and dependence are incompatible instinctions. So
are resentment and gratitude. So are self-hatred and the necessity to
exist as a self. By the time of his collapse, Mill's mental world apparently had become a mass of hopeless, unamalgamable contradictions. In effect he *was* his anarchic and inexpressible conflicts. During the autumn and winter months of 1826–1827, the swirling,
contradictive material that had been stimulated by the unresolvable
demands of his negative Oedipus complex at last subverted Mill's
sensibility. He seems to have become an organism capable only of
blocked fury and paralyzing contrition.

Emotional arrest and physical inaction apparently proposed themselves to Mill as a defense against his incommunicable and unacceptable contradictoriness. Because he could determine neither how to
feel nor how to act, he seems subliminally to have decided to feel
and to do nothing. He elected to sink into "a dull state of nerves."
He chose to become "insipid or indifferent," "without any real desire," "*blasé*" and capable of "no delight." This unconsciously deliberate self-extermination could quiet but it could not terminate Mill's
crippling confusions. Nor could it diminish his immobilizing sadness and pain. Only death—outright and absolute extermination—
seemed capable of concluding the "crisis." Mill's bitter conviction
that he "could not possibly bear" his subconsciously voluntary self-
annihilation "beyond a year" seems a sober and perhaps even an
overly sanguine assessment.

As Dr. Levi suggests, Mill's way of reading Marmontel's *Memoirs*
seems to have supplied him with a means by which to bring his
"mental malady" to a more satisfactory conclusion. The *Autobiography*'s account of the episode strongly supports Dr. Levi's theory that
Mill saw in the death of Marmontel's father a symbolization or a pre-
figuration of his own parent's death. Mill apparently imagined that
when James eventually died, all the enervating conflicts and confusions that inhered in his sonship would die as well. He seems to have

realized that when his father at last passed away, he would inherit a position of autonomy and authority equivalent to that which had devolved upon Marmontel.

I suggest that the prospect of his father's impending death excited Mill for another, even more stimulating reason. I believe Mill imagined that dying would adequately and appropriately punish his parent for having crippled his ability to experience "pleasurable excitement." Mill concluded, I believe, that *he* no longer needed consciously or unconsciously to hate his father and to seek retribution against him: for his father inevitably would be punished for his brutality and for his indifference in the same natural and absolute way that Marmontel's father had been punished. I believe that reading the *Memoirs* helped Mill rescue himself from the necessity to despise and from the necessity to avenge. Nature would, so to speak, avenge John. In time, in the due course of things, James must die, whether John wished him to die or whether he did not.

It is impossible to overestimate the importance of this discovery for Mill. I believe that this subconscious recognition allowed him for the first time in his life to risk having sensation. We have seen that Mill previously had not dared to experience conscious individualized emotions because he feared, correctly, that if he permitted himself to feel, he would feel rage. Reading the *Memoirs* helped him realize that he need never liberate his patricidal instincts. The *Memoirs* helped him realize that he could indefinitely sublimate his murderous anger, because the mandate or the mission of his anger eventually would accomplish itself.

Mill could not purge his fury. Nor could he exonerate himself for having felt fury. At least, though, he could exempt himself from ever having to become aware of his fury, and from ever having to act upon his fury. He could satiate his rage without every having either to comprehend or to contend with its unacceptable sources and its frightful meanings. Freed from his disabling fear that he one day might have to acknowledge and to serve his anger, Mill could risk experiencing his other, safer, sweeter emotions. He could tolerate partial awareness because he forever had banished the need to achieve complete awareness. Safely supressed, confidently domesticated, he could tolerate living as something more active and more interesting than "a stock or a stone."

But if all this were true, why did Mill weep? Why was he "moved to tears" when he read Marmontel's *Memoirs?* Why did he not laugh with happiness?

Mill himself believed that he wept because he compassionated. He declares in the *Autobiography* that he wept because he felt pity for Marmontel and for Marmontel's family. I suggest that he cried for another, much more personal reason. We have seen that the conception of his father's death as a symbolic punishment was extremely gratifying to Mill. But the idea of his father's death as a literal death must have been horrifying for him to contemplate. It is true that he subliminally resented James. But James remained both the source and the object of all the love that Mill ever had known. Despite the fact that he subconsciously hated his parent, Mill consciously adored him; and he continued to imagine that he could not survive without his father's support and care. It was chiefly for this reason, I believe,that Mill felt moved to tears when he read the *Memoirs*. He wept, I believe, in anticipatory grief for the death that the *Memoirs* encouraged him to envision. He wept because the experience he brought to the book caused him to recognize that in any number of crucial ways both his father and he himself must become destroyed by the death that his reading permitted him subrationally to foresee.

Mill probably wept for yet another reason. His reading almost certainly helped him realize that after his father's death he no longer would have to contend with the terrifying rage and guilt which his father had always made him feel. His father's death would desolate him. However, his father's death simultaneously would free him from the predicament that had structured his consciousness and precipitated his "crisis." Mill may have cried not only in anticipatory mourning, but also in anticipatory relief. He must have experienced a feeling of joy as he suddenly comprehended that he would not forever have to compel himself to be *"blasé,"* "insipid and indifferent"; that one day he might become able to liberate the sensations of gladness and confidence which more normally conditioned people believe they can afford to feel.

We are able to understand that this entire, intricate reaction to Marmontel's *Memoirs* was actually an abreaction. But Mill interpreted his response as a pure affect. He regarded his extraordinarily overdetermined manner of reading as an incontrovertible demonstration of the fact that he possessed the ability to feel independently and powerfully. It is an indication of how desperate his circumstances were that Mill needed to feel the wetness of his own tears to convince himself that he was human, and "not a stock or a stone."

In the context of this elemental desperation, Mill's malady must be regarded as a fortunate event. His "dejection" was intensely traumatic: without question the deep and protracted depression challenged his sanity and threatened his survival. Ultimately, though, the "crisis" forced Mill to think and to live in a healthier way. Specifically the "crisis" forced him to acknowledge and to repudiate the loneliness and the suffering that always before he had felt himself obliged to conceal and to accept. Mill's frightful "disease" (*Autobiography*, 81) momentarily arrested his development. It almost cost him his life. In the end, however, his disease made him comprehend that he could not permanently exist as "a mere reasoning machine" (*Autobiography*, 66). In the end it made him comprehend that he was a human being, and that he must live as a human being.[23]

In the *Autobiography*, Mill confirms the fact that his "mental crisis" produced "an important transformation in [his] opinions and character" (*Autobiography*, 80). He describes this "transformation" as consisting of two discrete but closely related changes in his "theory of life." He explains:

The experiences of this period had two very marked effects on my opinions and character. In the first place, they led me to adopt a theory of life, very unlike that on which I had before acted, and having much in common with what at that time I certainly had never heard of, the anti-self-consciousness theory of Carlyle. I never, indeed, wavered in the conviction that happiness is the test of all rules of conduct, and the end of life. But I now thought that this end was only to be attained by not making it the direct end. Those only are happy (I thought) who have their minds fixed on some object other than their own happiness; on the improvement of mankind, even on some art or pursuit, followed not as a means, but as itself an ideal end. Aiming thus at something else, they find happiness by the way. . . . Ask yourself whether you are happy, and you cease to be so. The only chance is to treat,

not happiness, but some end external to it, as the purpose of
life.

He continues:

> The other important change which my opinions at this time
> underwent, was that I, for the first time, gave its proper
> place, among the prime necessities of human well-being, to
> the internal culture of the individual. I ceased to attach al-
> most exclusive importance to the ordering of outward cir-
> cumstances, and the training of the human being for
> speculation and for action. I had now learnt by experience
> that the passive susceptibilities needed to be cultivated as
> well as the active capacities, and required to be nourished and
> enriched as well as guided. (*Autobiography*, 85–86)

Mill characterizes these new philosophies as persuasions that were
"very unlike" the ideas and the ideologies he had learned from his
father. It is true that in their broad outline his new "opinions" seem
distinctly to have differed from those he had been taught. James, we
recall, disparaged "happiness" and "the passive susceptibilities." He
"attached almost exclusive importance to the ordering of outward
circumstances." It was the sole purpose of his pedagogy to train "the
human being for speculation and for action." As we first read his
excited paragraphs, we accede to Mill's conviction that after surviv-
ing his "crisis" he significantly "transformed" his father's dreary and
deadening "theory of life."

When we examine the paragraph more closely, we discover that
Mill felt extremely ambivalent about the "transformation" he appears to celebrate. He speaks for "the internal culture of the individual." But he also, like his father, advances "anti-self-consciousness"
as an ideal.[24] He glorifies the power to feel. Yet his language, like
James's, is belligerently impersonal. Nouns of person occur in the
passage as if they represented kinds of machines or engines. He refers not to people or to minds or to hearts, but to such bloodless
abstractions as "human well-being," "the individual," and "the human being." He rarely speaks of himself or addresses us as a living,
desiring creature; he feels more comfortable referring to "my opinions and character." Whenever he does write the pronoun "I," he

seems to mean his philosophies, or the process of his mentation. The self that reasons and speaks in these paragraphs does not sound like the "internal," powerfully feeling, "nourished," "enriched" voice that it describes itself as being. Mill's imaginative revolution seems to have been conspicuously incomplete, and only partially acceptable to himself.

We may say more. As Mill recovered from his "crisis," it became his conscious intention to establish a "theory of life" that would at the same moment subvert and continue to defer to James's restrictive "opinion." It became Mill's deliberate purpose, he tells us, to syncretize rebellion with submission. In one of the *Autobiography's* most revealing passages, Mill declares:

> I did not, for an instant, lose sight of, or undervalue, that
> part of the truth which I had seen before; I never turned
> recreant to intellectual culture, or ceased to consider the
> power and practice of analysis as an essential condition both
> of individual and social improvement. But I thought that it
> had consequences which required to be corrected, by joining
> other kinds of cultivation with it. The maintaining of a due
> balance among the faculties, now seemed to me of primary
> importance. The cultivation of the feelings became one of the
> cardinal points in my ethical and philosophical creed. And
> my thoughts and inclinations turned in an increasing degree
> towards whatever seemed capable of being instrumental to
> that object. (*Autobiography*, 86)

"The maintaining of a due balance" between his parent's convictions and his own drives and desires became, I believe, Mill's principal psychological and artistic objective. Throughout his career he attempted to "correct" the "consequences" of his childhood without destroying the basal and irreplaceable affective structure that his childhood had imposed upon his imagination. In his thought and in his literature Mill tried to create a system of ideas and an arrangement of language—an exteriorized interiority—that would allow him to cultivate his own "feelings" without forcing him to feel consciously "recreant" to the "ethical and philosophical creed" upon which his emotions originally depended.

In the *Autobiography*, Mill reports that other men's literature, particularly Wordsworth's, defined and legitimized his new, more "balanced" consciousness. He asserts that Wordsworth's poetry became indispensable to his power to recover his health and his happiness. "What made Wordsworth's poems a medicine for my state of mind," Mill explains, "was that . . . they seemed to be the very culture of the feelings, which I was in quest of" (*Autobiography*, 89). I shall go on to suggest that it was not really Wordsworth's but rather his own literature that became Mill's "medicine." I shall suggest that Mill gradually controlled his despairs and his disorders by writing a long series of texts that indirectly expressed his deep ambivalence toward his father and his intense dissatisfaction with his father's "intellectual culture." I shall propose that in his artfully "balanced" essays, books, diaries, letters, and journals Mill created a mechanism which permitted him to simultaneously defy and deify the parent whom he both loved and loathed. I shall propose that by writing his complex, "joining" discourse, Mill symbolically accomplished the programme of his Oedipus complex and completed the work of his "mental crisis." In this sense, I shall contend, Mill's seemingly disinterested literature should be regarded not as a remote or an insensate public disquisition but as an intimate and a passionate experiment in personal therapy.

This has been a long and a complicated discussion. Before I address Mill's adult experience and his mature writings, it may be useful to review my conclusions about his infancy, childhood, and youth.

I have maintained that Mill's parents preserved an exhausted and a hostile marriage by treating their eldest child as a full participant in their severely strained relationship. Harriet Mill seems to have sustained her image of herself as an abused and silenced person by securing her son's contempt and disavowal. James Mill seems to have fulfilled his idea of himself as a regent and a god by co-opting his son's consciousness and by controlling virtually every aspect of his son's behavior. James required John to serve as his disciple and his vassal. He gradually came to regard his child less as a son than as a spouse. He seems to have viewed his child as a deferential and a brilliantly gifted replacement for the wife who had disappointed him by being unintelligent, ungainly, and dull. This was a role Mill accepted, relished, and wished to extend. His association with his father became a highly efficient, reciprocally gratifying alliance. For

his part Mill accepted the absolute authority, remoteness, and severity of his parent. He learned to conceive of himself as the essentially
nerveless instrument of his father's imperial will. In unconscious
gratitude and return, James conferred upon his son his time, his
affection, and his certifying regard.

This inversely organized Oedipal union provided significant compensations for Mill: few other sons ever have received from their fathers as much attention and as much esteem as this obedient boy
was able to command. However, the association also made for continual disappointment and dread. Mill could serve his father as
coadjutor and as sounding board. But he never could win the complete and explicit love that his father seemed always on the verge of
offering. Nor could he ever feel that his father loved or honored *him*.
Mill quickly discovered that he must suppress or kill the child who
he actually was in order that he might develop into the surrogate or
the symbol that his father needed him to become. Epically defense-
less, Mill did as he was bid. Self-effacement became his idiom. An
intense fear of self-knowledge became his ruling emotion. Denying
awareness became his controlling purpose.

Mill's self-suppression could not make his symbolizations become
real. No matter how many instincts, drives, desires, and functions
he sublimated or surrendered, he could not earn his parent's exclusive and expressed devotion. His relationship with his father was
substantiating and stimulating, but it was constitutionally limited:
the son never could become the sire's literal spouse. Mill bitterly resented the fact of his usurpation. At the same time, he bitterly resented the fact that his usurpation could not be made to become
more complete. Frustration and fury became his dominant feelings.

However, these feelings had to be concealed. In order to sustain
the inverted Oedipal mythology upon which his consciousness was
structured, Mill had to present to both his father and himself the
myth of his own contentment and completeness. Throughout his
childhood and youth, the need to express anger and the need not
to express anger intersected in Mill's subconscious intelligence.
These competing necessities created a fierce, seemingly unresolvable
conflict.

The tensions produced by this conflict seem to have precipitated
the celebrated "mental crisis" that afflicted Mill late in his delayed
and protracted adolescence. I have suggested that Mill recovered

from his life-threatening "malady" by constructing a sensibility that unconsciously expressed both his subversiveness and his submissiveness. This sensibility, I shall propose, lies at the heart of Mill's work, and at the heart of his continuing importance as a philosopher and as an artist.

John Mill was made something other than a self. Bonded to his parents by a whole set of unrelievable but not achievable yearnings, the Victorian civilization's most accomplished logical artist completed his adolescence and commenced his distinguished career in an internal condition of extreme dependency, doubt, and delusion. Libidinally an invalid, Mill brought to his manhood and to his seemingly supraliminal work the mentality with which he had been supplied as a son: a mentality ordered by acute fictitiousness, unconscious despair, and incipient hysteria.

To the behavior and to the literature that emerged from this gravely troubled psychology I now shall turn.

*—The necessity of personal collision
between one person and another is,
comparatively speaking, almost at an
end.*

_____**2**

Separation and Integration

During the ten years following his
"mental crisis," Mill consolidated and extended the attitudes and
the activities that seemed to him to have made the "essential condition" of his recovery from his "malady." He read widely in philosophies and in literatures that differed diametrically from his father's.
Particularly he studied the writings of Wordsworth, Coleridge, and
Comte. He organized a number of discussion and debating societies.
And he helped found and edit the *London Review* (later called the
London and Westminster Review). His efforts were not merely or solely
intellective. Mill worked assiduously to expand his social experience
and to develop his "passive susceptibilities." Especially he tried to
discover new people with whom he might associate. These experi-
ments were considerably successful. Mill gradually established intimate relationships with a number of the most distinguished men of
his own generation—Roebuck, Sterling, Graham, d'Eichthal, Tooke,
and, most notably, Carlyle. In 1831 he made the most important
friendship of his life. He met and fell in love with Harriet Taylor.[1]
Throughout this period Mill's development was primarily intra-

psychical: his "mental progress" (*Autobiography*, 111), as he later called it, was secret and virtually furtive. This seems to have been a deliberate choice. In 1833 he told Carlyle: "My occupations for some time have been rather internal than external. I have not been working much, but much has been working in me.² Mill did not completely conceal from his father or from his readers his new opinions, values, hopes, and loyalties. But he was careful to restrict his literature to issues and to concerns that did not dramatically conflict with his parent's. He confined his work to subjects in which he could intimate but not explicitly declare his evolving independence. In none of the many essays, articles, and reviews that he wrote during this period did he permit himself fully to describe his new attitude toward "the passive susceptibilities." Nor did he allow himself directly to criticize the limitations and the failures of his father's philosophies and methods.

Mill seems to have regarded these years as an era of voluntary suspension. He apparently thought of his life during this decade as a period of necessary and appropriate quiescence; a time in which he quietly and safely could explore his new convictions and feelings. In 1833 he wrote to Carlyle:

> I am often in a state almost of scepticism, and have no theory
> of Human Life at all, or seem to have conflicting theories, or
> a theory which does not amount to a Belief. This is only a
> *recent* state, and as I well know, a passing one, and my con-
> victions will be firmer and the result of a larger experience
> when I emerge from this state, than before.³

Four months later he optimistically declared: "Next year I shall probably be firmer on my legs, spiritually speaking, and shall have a clearer and more fixed insight into what I am to be and to do, than I have at present."⁴ Early in 1834 he told Carlyle: "There has taken place a great change in my character . . . —a change, not from any kind of *in*sincerity, but *to* a far higher kind of sincerity than belonged to me before."⁵ In the spring of 1834 he remarked:

> [I] have what for a considerable time was quite suspended in
> me, the 'feeling of growth.' I feel myself much more *knowing*,
> more *seeing*, having a far greater experience, of *realities*, not

abstractions, than ever before; nor do I doubt that this superior knowledge will make itself available in the form of a
greater power, for accomplishing whatever work I may be
called to, shall I say also for *chusing* the work which I most
worthily perform?[6]

It seemed crucial to Mill that, even as he cultivated this extraordinary "'feeling of growth'" he find some way to perpetuate the
"feeling" of his past experience—particularly the "feeling" that had
characterized his relationship with his father. In 1849 he told
Gustave d'Eichthal:

You probably have found out by experience as I have the
meaning of growing 'sadder & wiser' as one grows older &
that too without growing at all unhappy but on the contrary
happier. And you have felt as I have how one's course changes,
as one gets experience but changes by *widening* & therefore
keeps the same direction as before only with a slower movement as attempting to hit more points at once.[7]

Between 1826 and 1836, Mill tried to liberate himself from his ju-
venile dependency upon his father's "modes of thought and feeling."
But the liberation that he achieved was ambivalent, selective, and
extremely conservative. It seems that Mill regarded "the great change
in [his] character" as a "kind of sincerity" in which he publicly preserved his lifelong "direction," but privately resisted and partially
outgrew his "feeling" of enthrallment and indenture. During these
years he did not attempt to create a revolution in his sensibility. He
tried to encourage a process of continuous "*widening*": a process having as its object perpetual "transition" rather than definitive transformation. Mill apparently did not want to accomplish an insurrection
or a breakthrough. He seems rather to have desired to establish a
gradual, indefinite, and essentially harmless modification of his pre-
vailing consciousness.

This process of restrained "growth" eventually became for Mill a
public theme as well as a private intention. In 1831 he published a
series of essays entitled "The Spirit of the Age," in which he represented his individual experience of moderate evolution as a general
cultural phenomenon. In "The Spirit of the Age," Mill describes the

current state of society as a macroscopic version of his own "course."
He refers to the entire condition of English life in the nineteenth
century as a situation "pregnant with change"; as "an era of one of
the greatest revolutions of which history has preserved the remem-
brance, in the human mind, and in the whole constitution of society."[8] In a mood of both excitement and patience, he proclaims:
"The first of the leading peculiarities of the present age is, that it is
an age of transition. Mankind have outgrown old institutions and
old doctrines, and have not yet acquired new ones" (6).

Mill is careful to register concern, and even alarm, about this circumstance. He refers to the condition of "transition" as "not our
natural state" (12). He speaks cautiously—and with intimately personal intensity and meaning—of the lack of "authority" that afflicts
all people during such a period as "the present age." He remarks
that "the *natural* state of society, in respect of moral influence," must
always be, as it always was for himself, "that state in which the
opinions and feelings of the people are, with their voluntary acquiescence, formed *for* them, by the most cultivated minds which the
intelligence and the morality of the times call into existence" (41).
It seems to Mill inevitable and proper that, like himself, all people
ultimately should seek autonomy and "growth." But it is *"natural"*
and necessary, he contends, that, like himself, all men also should
try to find "persons to whom [they may] habitually defer, and in
whom they [may] trust for finding the right, and for pointing it
out." How this *"natural"* state might be achieved, either for himself
or for "the mass of the uninstructed" (41), did not seem to Mill possible to define in 1831. "The sequel of these papers," he declares,
"must be postponed." He could "resume [his] subject," he concluded, only at a later date—at some point "as early as possible after
the passing of the Reform Bill" (50).

The subjects of reference in "The Spirit of the Age" are manifest
and social. Mill is attempting to identify and to interpret phenomena that inhered in the consciousness of his community. Also,
though, the essay's concerns are symbolic and personal. Mill is trying to define and to analyze crucial transitional events in his own
consciousness. The "doctrines" that Mill personally was outgrowing
were his father's creeds and convictions. The "institutions" he indi-
vidually was abandoning were the subconscious needs that had led
him to grant these faiths excessive significance and authority. In

1831 it seemed to Mill that "the mass of the uninstructed" needed to liberate themselves from their society's old and exhausted "opinions and feelings." It seemed to Mill that he himself needed to become free of his father's worn-out opinions and feelings.

As we have seen, this freedom was not easy for Mill to achieve. He needed some large and revolutionary event to help him complete the "transition" he so painfully and so ambivalently had been trying to accomplish. During the winter of 1835–36, that event at last took place. While at the height of his powers and influence, James Mill became stricken with a series of debilitating pulmonary attacks. Throughout the spring of 1836 he was bedridden. On June 23, 1836, he died.

The problems that James's death created for Mill—the problems of loneliness, grief, confusion, and guilt—were numerous, terrifying, and temporarily unsolvable. Mill felt fully conscious about the extremity of his new situation. To d'Eichthal he wrote: "There is certainly something in a father's death (quite independent of personal affection) more solemn & affecting than any other loss. It closes the past, & as it were severs the connection between oneself and one's youth."[9]

As might be expected, Mill reacted to his loss very violently; and, initially, very self-destructively. He suffered a number of apparently sympathetic pulmonary episodes of his own.[10] He complained of incapacitating stomach pains. He developed symptoms of migraine headache. He produced a severe and, finally, a chronic twitching in his right eye. Most alarming of all, he sank into a protracted period of deep depression. Carlyle's description of Mill's condition a month after James's death is shocking. After returning from a visit to the Mills' home at Mickleham, Carlyle wrote:

> There was little sorrow visible in their house, or rather none, nor any human feeling at all; but the strangest *unheimlich* kind of composure and aquiescence, as if all human spontaneity had taken refuge in invisible corners. Mill himself talked much, and not stupidly—far from that—but without any emotion of any discernible kind. He seemed to me withered into the miserablest metaphysical *scrae*, body and mind, that I had almost every met with in the world. His eyes go twinkling and jerking with wild lights and twitches; his head

is bald, his face brown and dry. . . . Alas, poor fellow! It
seems possible too that he may not be very long seeable: that
is one way of its ending.[11]

Ultimately Mill found a healthier way of resolving his grief and
his terror. Despite his overwhelming senses of sorrow and rupture,
he eventually became able to experience his new circumstances as an
opportunity. The trauma of his loss and aloneness was monumental:
he had been suddenly and permanently deprived of the person who
had structured his entire sensibility. Yet he also had acquired an independence from that person. He had been granted an almost absolute freedom of movement and of mind. Mill knew that his father's
death was a "solemn & affecting" calamity. But he also gradually
recognized that his father's death had presented him with precisely
that possibility of autonomy which he had foreseen during his terrible "mental malady" in 1826.

As spring passed into summer, Mill became progessively more
excited about the new reality which he confronted. In November
1836, he wrote to Lytton Bulwer:

> As good may be drawn out of evil—the event which has
> deprived the world of the man of the greatest philosophic
> genius it possessed, and [*The London Westminster Re-
> view*] . . . of its most powerful writer, and the only one to
> whose opinions the editors were bound to defer—that same
> event has made it far easier to do that in hope of which alone
> I allowed myself to become connected with the review,
> namely to soften the harder and sterner features of its Radi-
> calism and Utilitarianism, both of which in the form in
> which they originally appeared in the *Westminster* were part of
> the inheritance of the eighteenth century.[12]

This idea of an acutely painful ultimate "good" resulting from his
father's death seems powerfully to have stimulated Mill. During the
autumn of 1836 and the winter of 1837, he recovered his health;
and slowly, most impressively, he recovered his spirits. In a condition of persisting shock but also of cautious, continually evolving excitement, Mill moved forward to engage his work and to experiment
with his liberty. Throughout these months, in each of his efforts as

an editor, an agitator, and a writer, he manfully tried to accomplish that "softening" of his father's "harder and sterner" features which it had become his choice as well as his "inheritance" to undertake.

Mill could not immediately reduce or perhaps even importantly challenge the centrality of his parent in his consciousness. However, he did begin to construct a body of work which transformed the corrosive consequences of that overidentification into a science and into an art which had the broadest possible imaginative utility for himself and for his society. In the months following his father's death, Mill began to live and to write within his own genius. In his thirtieth year, he commenced in earnest his extraordinary attempt to convert his pathologies into health, his confusions into insights, and his reactions—or his abreactions—into liberty and invention. The celebrated work that Mill produced after 1836 advanced itself as the terrain upon which he at last could contend with and satisfy his profound longing to love and to become loved. In this respect, as we shall see, the seemingly soulless literature of John Stuart Mill eventually organized itself into one of the most individualistic, sensual, and urgent literatures ever written by any father's son.

Mill's first formal reaction to his father's death was anticipatory. Two months before James died, Mill published an essay entitled "Civilization." The essay proposes itself as a dispassionate analysis of "Man and Society . . . [in] our time"; an objective account of the advantages and "the vices or the miseries" that constitute "the irresistible consequences of a state of advancing civilization." [13] This is a large and a fascinating theme. But it is not, I believe, "Civilization"'s primary subject. As he consciously engaged the essay's compelling public issues, Mill unconsciously confronted other, for himself more immediate questions. He tried to identify "the irresistible consequences" of his father's impending death. Particularly he tried to determine to what extent he might distinguish between his relationship with his father and his socialization as a whole; to what extent he might distinguish between his approaching independence and absolute aloneness; and to what extent he might distinguish between his evolving autonomy and the threat of imaginative and libidinal anarchy. In the months before his parent's death, Mill seems to have prepared for his loss by creating a circumspect, thoroughly displaced discussion of the powerful anxieties that the imminent

revolution in his circumstances was causing him to feel. He appears
to have responded to the "irresistible" fact of his excitement and his
desolation by trying to represent his radically conflicted hopes, joys,
inhibitions, and hysterias as "vices" and "miseries" inherent in "the
characteristic features of our time."

The essay opens with a brief and striking account of the nature
and the history of civilization. Mill suggests that civilization is necessary and invaluable, but that it is a blessing which causes numerous consequences. He declares:

> We hold that civilization is a good, that it is the cause of
> much good, and is not incompatible with any; but we think
> that there is other good, much even of the highest good,
> which civilization does not provide for, and some which it
> has a tendency (though that tendency may be counteracted)
> to impede. (51)

Civilization is "the cause of much good," Mill believes, because it
compels human beings to unify, to produce, and to achieve advances. Mill especially admires the ability of civilized people to pool
their resources and their talents. "There is not a more accurate test of
civilization," he remarks, "than the progress of the power of cooperation" (55). As we learn to cooperate, Mill observes, we learn to perform differing functions with increasing and increasingly specialized
skill. Equally important, we learn to exteriorize and to domesticate
our potentially destructive instincts. Especially we learn broadly and
equitably to share the experiences and the privileges of authority. In
primitive periods in a people's development, Mill reminds us, there
exists an "utmost excess of poverty or impotence in the masses;
[and] the enormous importance and uncontrollable power of a small
number of individuals, each of whom, within his own sphere, knew
neither law nor superior" (54). He continues:

> In savage life, . . . every one trusts to his own strength or
> cunning, and where that fails he is without resource. We ac-
> cordingly call a people civilized, where the arrangements of
> society, for protecting the persons and property of its mem-
> bers . . . induce the bulk of the community to rely for their
> security mainly upon the social arrangements, and renounce

for the most part, and in ordinary circumstances, the vindication of their interests (whether in the way of aggression or defense) by their individual strength or courage. (52–53)

This renunciation, Mill contends, is crucial to our power to live in continuity and in confidence. As we grow more capable of repudiating personal "strength or cunning," as we learn to surrender individual aggressiveness, "the bulk of the community" becomes capable of enjoying highly increased productivity and pleasure. All civilized people eventually must learn, Mill proclaims, "the *value* of combination; they [must] see how much and with what ease it accomplishes, [that] which never could be accomplished without it" (57).

This great and indispensable "accomplishment" exacts, however, a terrible price. It seems to Mill that as people become more capable of "submitting themselves to guidance, and subduing themselves to act as interdependent parts of a complex whole" (57), they gradually forfeit "energy of character" (63). In one of the essay's most prescient passages, Mill declares:

> One of the effects of a high state of civilization upon character, is a relaxation of individual energy. . . . In a rude state, each man's personal security, the protection of his family, his property, his liberty itself, depend greatly upon his bodily strength and his mental energy or cunning: in a civilized state, all this is secured to him by causes extrinsic to himself. . . . Compared with former times, there is in the refined classes of modern civilized communities much more of the amiable and humane, and much less of the heroic. (63, 65)

Mill believes that this is especially true of his own age. In the contemporary era, he remarks:

> There is a great increase of humanity, a decline of bigotry, and of many of the repulsive qualities of aristocracy, among our conspicuous classes; but there is, to say the least, no increase of shining ability, and a very marked decrease of vigour and energy. With all the advantages of this age, its facilities for mental cultivation, the incitements and the rewards

which it holds out to excited talents, there can scarcely be
pointed out in the European annals any stirring times, which
have brought so little that is distinguished, either morally or
intellectually, to the surface. (59)

Mill concludes: "there has crept over the refined classes, over the
whole class of gentlemen in England, a moral effeminacy, an inaptitude for every kind of struggle" (65).

Mill believes that this creeping "effeminacy" constitutes the great
crisis of modern life. He concludes that this crisis is endemic to civilization. He declares: "This torpidity and cowardice, as a general
characteristic, is new in the world: but (modified by the different
temperaments of different nations) it is a natural consequence of the
progress of civilization, and will continue until met by a system
of cultivation adapted to counteract it" (66). The only "system of
cultivation" that Mill believes can "counteract" the vitiating effects
of civilization is a new liberalism in education. He feels certain that
the contemporary English civilization must reorganize its concept of
education and its methods of pedagogy. He passionately advances
the belief that his civilization must inculcate and protect perfect liberty of thought. He insists that it is particularly necessary to protect
individual citizens' ability and right to create independent or even
subversive thought. He implores us to believe in the necessity and
the beauty of individualism, even as we believe in and serve the
equally compelling claims of "combination" and "community."

Mill wants, characteristically, to revise reality in such a way as to
both perpetuate and alter the fundamental conditions of human experience. He wants to "counteract" the "natural consequence of the
progress of civilization" at the same moment that he communes
with, contributes to, and thus reinforces the claims of civilization.
Throughout the essay, he attempts to incorporate and to adjust
rather than to deconstruct and to originate. He yearns to reinvigo-
rate rather than to build something wholly different and entirely
new. Throughout "Civilization," as throughout his life, Mill feels
impelled to speak simultaneously on behalf of and against "causes
extrinsic to himself." He moves instinctively to reject *and* to accept
everything in life which inhibits "bodily strength" and "mental energy or cunning."

These are the conscious themes and intentions of "Civilization." There is, however, a hidden, subliminal discourse which establishes itself within the deliberate and the aware writing. As I suggested earlier, I believe that Mill conceals in "Civilization" a more subjective and a more passionate essay: an essay in which he examines and attempts to relieve his own condition of "moral effeminacy" and "inaptitude," his individual failure of "the heroic." I believe this because many of Mill's phrases and paragraphs seem very oddly and certainly very excitedly charged. His choices of words, styles, and tones frequently expose grossly overdetermined, distinctly personal attitudes and convictions. His uses of language strongly suggest that as he wrote "Civilization," Mill subconsciously was thinking about and referring to events and emotions in his own life.

This seems especially true of Mill's descriptions of civilization itself. Throughout the essay he discusses the characteristics of culture and community in such a way as to imply that he unconsciously is investigating his personal experience of socialization. Let us consider again his descriptions of civilization's origins, purposes, and consequences. Mill delares, we recall, that progress in "cooperation" involves every human being in a certain unwilled and unacknowledged co-optation. In order to acquire the achievements, the securities, and the pleasures that civilization confers, men must learn "the practical lesson of submitting themselves to guidance, and subduing themselves to act as interdependent parts of a complex whole" (57). This "subduing" seems to Mill a highly ambivalent phenomenon. He repeatedly emphasizes in the essay that "one of the effects of a high state of civilization upon character, is a relaxation of individual energy" (63). Will, cunning, strength, and ardency all appear to Mill to be significantly deteriorating in the modern world. It seems to him that at the present moment "the individual becomes so lost in the crowd, that . . . an established character becomes at once more difficult to gain, and more easily to be dispensed with" (67). So, too, Mill believes, has "established," authentic experience become "more difficult to gain." He comments:

There is another circumstance to which we may trace much both of the good and of the bad qualities which distinguish our civilization from the rudeness of former times. One of the

effects of civilization (not to say one of the ingredients in it),
is that the spectacle, and even the very idea of pain, is kept
more and more out of the light of those classes who enjoy in
their fulness the benefits of civilization. The state of perpetual
personal conflict rendered necessary by the circumstances of
all former times, and from which it was hardly possible for
any person, in whatever rank of society to be exempt, necessarily habituated every one to the spectacle of harshness,
rudeness, and violence, to the struggle of one indomitable
will against another, and to the alternate suffering and inflic-
tion of pain. . . . The necessity of personal collision between
one person and another is, comparatively speaking, almost at
an end. (64–65)

This "effect of civilization" appears to Mill to be producing a "revolution" in the circumstances, and therefore in the condition itself, of
being human. He observes:

The change which is thus in progress, and to a great extent
consummated, is the greatest ever recorded in human affairs;
the most complete, the most fruitful in consequence, and the
most irrevocable. . . . So great a revolution vitiates all existing rules of government and policy, and renders all practice
and all predictions grounded only upon previous experience
worthless. . . . The whole face of society is reversed—all
the natural elements of power have definitively changed
places. . . . Whatever is the growing power in society will
force its way into the government, by fair means or foul. The
distribution of constitutional power cannot continue very
different from that of real power, without a convulsion.
(59–60)

This is anything but neutral commentary. Barely concealed within
the seemingly dispassionate analysis is a passionate oratory: an oratory about "strength," "cunning," "energy," and "will"; an oratory
about "security," "aggression," and "defence"; an oratory about "impotence," "compromise," "subduing"; an oratory about "harshness,"
"violence," "struggle," and "collision"; an oratory about, above all
else, "sacrifice," "suffering," and "pain." The incompletely conscious

theme of "Civilization" seems to be power. Mill really is writing about the ways in which human beings claim and yield authority. He is discussing the means by which "the bulk of the community"—or, I believe, he himself—may achieve the right, the "will," and the ability freely to desire and freely to act.

In this context, it is likely that the "sphere" to which the essay primarily refers is not "Man and Society" so much as Mill's own family. All the passages which I have cited suggest that as he was writing "Civilization" Mill subconsciously was reflecting upon and attempting to change the specific "arrangements of society" that existed between his father and himself. As we read his remarks about society and culture, we hear a deflected but nevertheless a bold and distinctive commentary upon Mill's experiences of boyhood, education, and discipleship. When he speaks of "the savage state," we hear a discourse upon his feelings about his impoverished and imperiled condition as a child. He seems to be unconsciously discussing "the utmost excess of poverty and impotence" in himself and "the enormous importance and uncontrollable power" of his parent. When he speaks of "the progress of the power of co-operation" and the necessity of "submitting . . . to guidance," when he speaks of the immense "sacrifice" and the incalculable benefits that are entailed by "combination," he seems to be meditating upon the period or the era of his intensely stimulating but acutely painful education. When he speaks of civilized persons' "subduing themselves to act as inter-dependent parts of a complex whole," when he speaks of the awful "compromises" inherent in communal associations, he seems to be soliloquizing upon the difficult years of his apprenticeship as a junior Utilitarian.

In these respects "Civilization" unconsciously concerns Mill's past. However, the essay's principal subconscious purpose is to engage the future—mankind's future, and the author's own. Throughout "Civilization," Mill publicly examines the revolutionary changes that seemed to him to be at hand for society. He privately considers the changes that were at hand for himself. As he wrote "Civilization," his awesome father was about to die. For Mill, "the change which [was] thus in progress, and to a great extent consummated" seemed unquestionably "the greatest ever recorded" in at least his own "human affairs; the most complete, the most fruitful in consequences, and the most irrevocable." The entire topography of his existence

was about to be transformed. Everything having to do with necessity, value, and possibility had become an open issue for Mill. His
father's death seemingly would cause "the whole face of society" to
redefine and to reorder itself. "All the natural elements of power"
would abruptly and "definitively [change] places." Precisely because
"so great a revolution [would vitiate] all existing rules" of Mill's internal "government and policy," he needed to accept and to explore
the meanings of the fact that "the distribution of constitutional
power" was now, at last, completely in his own control.

I believe that "Civilization" presented itself to Mill as a grand,
syncretized expression of the state of his own affairs in 1836. The
essay addresses a cognition of crisis and of opportunity: a crisis and
an opportunity which seemed to Mill at once personal and public, of
the self and of the society.

The opportunity Mill especially needed to comprehend and to develop was the opportunity for tranquility which was about to become available to him. As his father lay dying, Mill seems subconsciously to have realized that happiness, confidence, and peace were
within his reach. The dreadful "struggle of one indomitable will
against another," the grotesque "necessity of personal collision between one person and another" finally was ending. "The state of perpetual personal conflict, rendered necessary by the circumstances of
all former times" was about to become conclusively concluded.

As we have seen, Mill reacted to this transforming event with
honorable ambivalence. He welcomed his impending liberation. He
delighted in the fact that now he might legitimately sublimate the
confusion and the pain which throughout his earlier years he had
tried surreptitiously to suppress. He delighted in the fact that, like
other modern people, he now could appropriately "keep out of the
light" the "very idea of pain," the whole "spectacle of harshness,
rudeness, and violence" which had characterized his childhood and
his youth. At the same time, he lamented the loss of certain elements of his "prior experience." He knew that when his father died
there also must perish much, if not everything, he ever before had
known about love, order, value, and purpose. Mill exulted in his
imminent release from conflict and confusion. He reveled in his opportunity at last to become civilized. But he also longed to remain
in the state of "savage life." He longed to perpetuate the feelings of
coherence and certainty which had been the consolation of his years

of misery. Mill took pleasure in the possibility of finally becoming able, like other socialized persons, to achieve an "established character." But he feared the loneliness and the chaos that he believed must descend upon his psyche when he lost his parent's "guidance."

Mill resolved his ambivalence by accepting and systematizing it. He concluded "Civilization" and solved the crisis that led him to write the essay by identifying a principle of existence that could simultaneously separate and unite his father and himself. This was a momentous occasion for Mill, and he created a momentous tone to express his emotions of seriousness and gladness. "The great business of every rational being," he proclaims, is "the strengthening and enlarging of his own intellect" (74). Every human being, he declares, "should go forth determined and qualified to seek truth ardently, vigorously, and disinterestedly."

The genius of these exclamations lies in their broadness. The testaments and the ethos they subliminally define provide an ultimate sanction for both the father's and the son's behaviors. Mill subconsciously is declaring that his father may have been oppressive and perhaps even belligerent as a parent and as a teacher. However, Mill concludes, his father meant only to equip him to pursue "the great business" of life. Mill himself may have seemed ungrateful and unloving. But he meant only to complete his parent's vision and to serve civilization. In effect, Mill is stating: my father loved me well, and I may love him. It is appropriate and loving, it is supremely civilized to want "to seek truth" of my own. Indeed, my father would want me to separate from him. My father would want me to employ the sensibility and the skills he gave me to liberate myself from his convictions, and to make myself independent of his ways of being. "Strengthening and enlarging" my own intelligence and character really should be regarded as a fulfillment of my father's hopes and plans. Seen from the proper point of view, seen from the point of view of civilization, the most loving and the most loyal thing I can do for my parent is to free myself from his "government." If I comprehend and love my parent, if I comprehend and love civilization, I "should go forth": I should seek and achieve a new, more liberal, more personal "distribution of constitutional power."

Mill finds a more abstract but an equally forceful way to express and to celebrate these conclusions. In a mood of extreme but, characteristically, extremely controlled excitement, he writes:

The very corner-stone of an education intended to form great minds must be the recognition of the principle, that the object is to call forth the greatest possible quantity of intellectual *power*, and to inspire the intensest *love of truth*; and this without a particle of regard to the results to which the exercise of that power may lead, even though it should conduct the pupil to opinions diametrically opposite to those of his teachers. . . . We are not so absurd as to propose that the teacher should not inculcate his own opinions as the true ones, and exert his utmost powers to exhibit their truth in the strongest possible light. To abstain from this would be to nourish the worst intellectual habit of all, that of not finding, and not looking for, certainty in anything. (80–81)

His father, Mill is suggesting, fulfilled his "business" and his "truth" superbly well: he "inculcated his opinions . . . in the strongest light." Now, as his "pupil," his heir, and his beloved son, Mill himself must "go forth" and fulfill his own more modern, although perhaps mutinous truth. Mill recognizes that this is not only his deepest personal desire but also his "great business" as a man. Mill is deciding that, interpreted in the context of civilization, separation really is evolution. Independence really is continuity and unification.

In "Civilization" we are made witness to a critically important moment in Mill's life. We are permitted to share in the precise instant in which he consciously realizes that he has no occasion to feel either remorse or sorrow. We are allowed to participate in the very processes of thought and will by which this extraordinarily loving son recognizes that, seen from the vantage point offered by the ideals of culture, his longing to individualize himself should be regarded neither as an act of defiance nor of "conflict" nor of "collision," but rather as an act of holy communion with his father, with society, and with life itself.

Mill's final treatment of this theme in "Civilization" is confident and joyful. He seems to have felt thoroughly aware of the fact that he at last had achieved the possibility of release from his "prior experience." Equally important, he seems to have understood that he had accomplished a remarkable feat of socialization. He seems to have realized that he had discovered a means by which he might unite his own strange and isolated experience, insights, and "business" with the needs and the purposes of more ordinary people. With great decisiveness and unmistakable pleasure, he declares:

> Those advantages which civilization cannot give—which in
> its uncorrected influence it has even a tendency to destroy—
> may yet coexist with civilization; and it is only when joined
> to civilization that they can produce their fairest fruits. All
> that we are in danger of losing we may preserve, all that we
> have lost we may regain, and bring to a perfection hitherto
> unknown; but not by slumbering, and leaving things to
> themselves, no more than by ridiculously trying our strength
> against their irresistible tendencies: only by establishing
> counter-tendencies, which may combine with those tenden-
> cies, and modify them. (71)

Mill is defining here both a general and a personal "truth." His public injunction is obvious, even simplistic. He is stating that civilized people must nourish everything which has been valuable about their past, even as they confront "the necessity . . . that we should adopt many new rules, and new courses of action" (52). For himself Mill is decreeing a far more complex and a far more inventive policy. He is expressing his intention to synthesize his old, overdetermined will to preserve the past with his new, much more creative determination to construct a future. He is proclaiming that he will cherish and sustain everything in his relationship with his father that has been wholesome, useful, and loving; but that he will emancipate himself from everything in that primal interaction that has been inimical to and destructive of his "individual energy."

The terms of this resolution were profoundly attractive to Mill and completely in keeping with the structure of his consciousness. He chooses coexistence and combination rather than confrontation. He embraces modification and adjustment rather than conflict and destruction. This spirit of gentle and generous accommodation became the "corner-stone" of Mill's final response to his father. It became as well the "corner-stone" of his individualization and his art. To "preserve" the most usable elements of his "prior experience" and to establish "counter-tendencies" to those materials he could not utilize seemed to him to be the most effective means by which he could survive and build upon his father's death. For the rest of his life this cautious, compromised "revolution," this ethic of quietistic revision, seemed to Mill to propose itself as the wisest approach to existence's "fairest fruits." The policy seemed to guarantee, indeed, "a perfection hitherto unknown" for himself and for the human community at large.

"Civilization" is a most important essay for the light it sheds upon the social problems and the social sciences of the nineteenth century. The essay also is important because of its exceptional significance in Mill's own moral and imaginative development. Writing "Civilization" appears to have stimulated Mill to "interrogate his own consciousness, to cherish and experiment upon himself" (83). As he wrote the essay, Mill seems to have concluded that only by "experimenting" upon his thoughts and opinions could "the infinite varieties of human nature be so vividly brought home to him, and anything cramped or one-sided in his own standard of it be so effectually corrected" (82). He seems to have realized that only by "interrogating his own consciousness" could he "behold so strikingly exemplified the astonishing pliability of our nature, and the vast effects which may under good guidance be produced upon it by honest human endeavour" (82). In "Civilization," Mill authorized and liberated a decision to become more completely alive. As he thought and wrote during the most trying days of his life, he identified, justified, and began to accomplish the primary impulse of his imagination: the impulse to create "an established character." For this reason "Civilization" reads less as a disinterested sociology than as a highly personal and an intensely excited apologia—a tentative prolegomenon to a not yet written autobiography.

I have given extensive attention and considerable enthusiasm to a work that may seem to some readers unremarkable and perhaps even uninteresting. I have done so because "Civilization" seems to me to constitutue a landmark in Mill's life and the "corner-stone" of his career. As he conceived of and wrote this ardent essay, Mill mastered a primal emergency and established the foundation of his sensibility. He responded to the threat of desolation by deciding to survive, by deciding to be autonomous, and by deciding to be productive. In "Civilization," we are invited to observe an extraordinary moment: the moment in which a genius identified and embraced his instincts, his aspirations, and his immense abilities.

Mill returned to the subjects and the strategies of "Civilization" in "Bentham," an essay published in 1838. The essay identifies itself as a study of the mind, the methods, and the importance of Jeremy Bentham. Mill discusses Bentham as the hero of a certain kind of philosophical consciousness. He celebrates Bentham as his culture's foremost exponent and practitioner of disinterested criticism: as, in his famous phrase, "in this age and country the great questioner of things established." [14] This seems to Mill to constitute no small or narrow achievement. He believes that Bentham should be recognized as a unique and indispensable apostle of human freedom. He declares: "It is by the influence of the modes of thought with which his writings inoculated a considerable number of thinking men, that the yoke of authority has been broken, and innumerable opinions, formerly received upon opinion as incontestable, are put upon their defence and required to give an account of themselves" (87).

Nothing in this illustrious and fascinating essay is more important than Mill's use of the word "inoculated." The striking word suggests that Bentham's effect upon Mill and upon the other "thinking men" of nineteenth-century England was medicinal. It suggests, in fact, that Bentham identified and helped to cure a disease. The disease that Mill believes Bentham confronted is that failure in thought and in sensibility which attends upon a blind, enervating adherence to "authority." Bentham proposes himself to Mill as a heroic doctor-soldier, who combated "the united authority of the instructed" (87). Mill describes Bentham as a saintly healer-warrior, who struggled against the totems and taboos of a civilization that had been organized and presided over by shamans, seigneurs, and sorcerers. He writes:

> Until [Bentham] spoke out, those who found our institutions
> unsuited to them did not dare to say so, did not dare con-
> sciously to think so. . . . Bentham broke that spell. It was
> not Bentham by his own writings, it was Bentham through
> the minds and the pens which those writings fed—through
> the men in more direct contact with the world, into whom
> his spirit passed. If the superstition about ancestorial wisdom
> has fallen into decay; if the public are grown familiar with
> the idea that their laws and institutions are not the product of

intellect and virtue, but of modern corruption grafted upon
ancient barbarism; if the hardiest innovation is not scouted
because it is an innovation—establishments no longer considered sacred because they are establishments—it will be found
that those who have accustomed the public mind to these
ideas have learned them in Bentham's school, and that the
assault on ancient institutions has been, and is, carried on
for the most part with his weapons. . . . The father of English innovation, both in doctrines and in institutions, is
Bentham: he is the great *subversive*, or, in the language of
continental philosophers, the great *critical*, thinker of his age
and country. (87–88)

Mill believes that Bentham had an even more important virtue
than his subversiveness. It seems to him that, unlike "purely negative thinkers, [Bentham] was positive: they only assailed error, he
made it a point of conscience not to do so until he thought he could
plant instead the corresponding truth" (91). The distinction seems
to Mill to be of the utmost significance. He explains:

Their character was exclusively analytic, his was synthetic.
They took for their starting point the received opinion on any
subject, dug round it with their logical implements, pro-
nounced its foundations defective, and condemned it: he began *de novo*, laid his own foundations deeply and firmly, built
up his own structure, and bid mankind compare the two; it
was when he had solved the problem himself, or thought he
had done so, that he declared all other solutions to be erroneous. (91)

In this sense, Mill contends, Bentham was a creative artist, a con-
server rather than a destroyer. He comments:

What he did had its own value, by which it must outlast all
errors to which it is opposed. Though we may reject, as often
we must, his practical conclusions, yet his premises, the col-
lections of facts and observations from which his conclusions
were drawn, remain for ever, a part of the materials of philosophy. (91–92)

It is for this reason more than any other that Mill admires and feels affection for Bentham. He concludes:

> He was not a great philosopher, but he was a great reformer in philosophy. . . . He introduced into morals and politics those habits of thought and modes of investigation, which are essential to the idea of science; and the absence of which made those departments of inquiry, as physics had been before Bacon, a field of interminable discussion, leading to no result. It was not his *opinions* in short, but his *method,* that constituted the novelty and the value of what he did; a value beyond all price, even though we should reject the whole, as we unquestionably must a large part, of the opinions themselves. (92)

This is, as always with Mill, singularly complicated discourse. He celebrates Bentham. At the same time, however, he indicts him. He proclaims that Bentham was both an invaluable and an invalid thinker. He tells us that we must enthusiastically appreciate Bentham's intentions and methods; but that we also must repudiate his views and conclusions. He contends that we must admire and use everything in Bentham's philosophy that has a "value"; but that we also must "reject" everything that is excessive or inelegant or "erroneous." Once again Mill experiences and expresses extreme ambivalence. Once again he accepts and systematizes his ambivalence. He concludes that it is necessary to react in opposing ways to his subject. He insists that the only appropriate response we can make to Bentham is a mixed if not a contradictory response. As he had done in "Civilization," Mill wants to synthesize conflicting opinions and feelings. He wants, it appears, to discover a means by which he may simultaneously unite himself with and separate himself from one of the sovereign sensibilities of his "age and country."

We cannot help but feel aware at this point of a circumstance that must have been very much in Mill's mind as he conceived of and wrote "Bentham." Bentham was, of course, the founder and the leader of that school of thought in which Mill himself had been educated. Moreover, Bentham was James Mill's closest friend and associate. As I suggested earlier, Bentham and James Mill virtually were partners; the two men almost were coessential with one another. Mill himself viewed the relationship that existed between his father and Bentham less as a partnership than as a somewhat parasitic symbiosis—a symbiosis in which James Mill, not Bentham, was the host or the dominant figure. In the *Autobiography*, Mill goes so far as to declare:

> The notion that Bentham was surrounded by a band of disciples who received their opinions from his lips is a fable. . . . The influence which Bentham exercised was by his writings. . . . But my father exercised a far greater personal ascendancy.

Mill acknowledges that Bentham "is a much greater name in history." But he states clearly and firmly that "it was my father's opinions which gave the distinguishing character to the Benthamic or utilitarian propagandism of that time." [15] In "Bentham," Mill again expresses his conviction that his father was not only Bentham's colleague and coadjutor but also his complementary superior. He observes:

> We must not look for subtlety, or the power of recondite analysis, among [Bentham's] intellectual characteristics. In the former quality, few great thinkers have been so deficient; and to find the latter, in any considerable measure, in a mind acknowledging any kindred with his, we must have recourse to the late Mr. Mill—a man who united all the great qualities of the metaphysicians of the eighteenth century, with others of a different complexion, admirably qualifying him to complete and correct their work. Bentham had not these particular gifts; but he had others, not inferior, which were not possessed by any of his precursors; which have made him a source of light to a generation which has far outgrown their influence. (89–90)

This is, I believe, the central passage of "Bentham." Certainly it is one of the most important paragraphs Mill ever wrote—one of the most important, at least, in the terms of his personal evolution. Mill is indicating here that in his conscious discussion of Bentham he subconsciously has imagined and referred to his father. He has intended to describe "the distinguishing character" of both men. He has meant to define in what respects Jeremy Bentham and "the late Mr. Mill" achieved "value," and therefore deserve to be honored and followed; and in what respects the two "Benthamic or utilitarian" philosophers failed, and deserve to be "rejected."

The key phrases in this, for Mill, very bold paragraph are "the late Mr. Mill" and "a generation which has far outgrown their influence." The two phrases communicate two major developments in Mill's subliminal thought. Mill is acknowledging, first, that "the late Mr. Mill" has died. "Mr. Mill" may be discussed, loved, adhered to, or repudiated. He continues to have the power to influence and to inspire. But no longer can "Mr. Mill" obligate or compel. His "intellectual authority" at last has come to an end. This situation, Mill goes on to suggest, is at once individual and generational. "The late Mr. Mill" and Jeremy Bentham belonged, Mill declares, to the eighteenth century. Their ideas, values, and styles were manifestations of a discrete era as well as creations of two discrete personalities. The two great eighteenth-century thinkers may be regarded as "a source of light." No longer, however, can they command absolute "authority."

This recognition constitutes a separation. For the commentator, John Mill, was conspicuously one of the leading men of the "generation which has far outgrown" the "influence" of its archaic precursors. Mill is asserting that it is responsible and necessary for the new, more modern men—for the sons—to develop new methods and new views; new "subtlety" in "recondite analysis" and in primary life. It is feasible and right for John Mill and his contemporaries "to complete and correct" Mr. Mill's and Jeremy Bentham's "outmoded" philosophies and outmoded characters. Properly understood, this act of revision will be neither personal nor impious. Rather, it will be an act of civilized "criticism," a rehabilitation rather than a rebellion.

Mill is completing here a crucial phase in his imaginative evolution. He is identifying those respects in which his mentors warrant his love and his communion. He also is identifying those respects in which his mentors deserve, and will excuse, his defection. We may characterize his achievement more precisely. In "Bentham," Mill considerably expanded the psychological work he began in "Civilization." He further delineated the ideological ground on which he could justify terminating his father's power to dominate his emotions and to control his behaviors.

In the passage we have been reading, Mill accomplished another, far more significant advance. As he created his identification of Bentham and his father, he managed inversely but decisively to identify himself. After all, only a person who essentially was not like his "precursors" could discern and describe his precursors' limitations. As he defined the specific failures of the men who had formed him, Mill at last defined the specific content of his differences from Bentham and "the late Mr. Mill." As he recognized the particular inadequacies of his intimidating teachers, he at last commenced to recognize and to value the particular properties of his own character and consciousness.

The qualities and capabilities that Mill began to realize were peculiarly his own were those associated with affect, or with feeling. Throughout the essay he suggests that the principal weakness of Jeremy Bentham and, by extension, of James Mill, was their shared inability to experience and to appreciate emotions. In a mood of solemn sadness, Mill declares:

> In many of the most natural and strongest feelings of human nature [Bentham] had no sympathy; from many of its graver experiences he was altogether cut off; and the faculty by which one mind understands a mind different from itself, and throws itself into the feelings of that other mind, was denied him, by his deficiency of Imagination. (103)

He continues:

> Bentham's knowledge of human nature is bounded. It is wholly empirical; and the empiricism of one who has had little experience. He had neither internal experience nor external; the quiet, even tenor of his life, and his healthiness of mind, conspired to exclude him from both. . . . How much of human nature slumbered in him he knew not, neither can we know. He had never been made alive to the unseen influences which were acting on himself, nor consequently on his fellow-creatures. . . . He measured [all men] but by one

standard; their knowledge of facts, and their capability to take correct views of utility, and merge all other objects in it. (104)

This is extremely important material. Mill is declaring that his "precursors" failed to develop precisely that "experience" in which he himself excelled: the ability to create, to comprehend, and to treasure "feelings." What is more, Mill is declaring that Bentham and "the late Mr. Mill" failed as philosophers and as persons exactly because of their "quiet, even tenor," their great "healthiness of mind." He is suggesting that if Bentham and James Mill had felt more pain, if they had, like himself, confronted confusion, conflict, and disorder, they might have achieved a deeper insight into "the unseen influences" that define and shape human life. As he wrote "Bentham," Mill was moving to incorporate and to sanction his "mental crisis" of 1822. He was trying, I believe, to represent his personal "tenor" of anxiety and anguish as the basis of an original and an appropriately modern "healthiness of mind." He was trying to recognize his own peculiar experience, his own seeming lack of health, as a new, a valid, and a vastly promising instrument for contemporary philosophy.

In writing "Bentham," Mill unconsciously was attempting to complete his evolution from infancy into adulthood. In order to accomplish this difficult but necessary transition, he had decisively to separate himself from his father's temperament and values. In this context, his final judgments about the Utilitarians' "deficiency of Imagination" are most significant. As he concluded "Bentham," Mill allowed himself to understand that the Benthamic philosophy and "character" was "bounded" especially by its failures of passion. He permitted himself to perceive that the most serious limitation that afflicted his mentors' minds was their inability to feel love. In a state of barely contained anger, Mill declares:

Man, that most complex being, is a very simple one in [Bentham's] eyes. Even under the head of *sympathy*, his recognition does not extend to the more complex forms of the feeling—the love of *loving*, the need of a sympathising support, or of an object of admiration and reverence. If he thought at all of any of the deeper feelings of human nature,

it was as but idiosyncrasies of taste, with which neither the
moralist nor the legislator had any concern, further than to
prohibit such as were mischievous among the actions to
which they might chance to lead. (107)

This "deficiency" seems to Mill to have produced in the Benthamic
"character" terrible limitations and perversions. In what I think is
the most manifestly melancholy passage he ever composed, Mill
observes:

> [Bentham's] own lot was cast in a generation of the leanest
> and barrenest men whom Europe had yet produced, and he
> was an old man when a better race came in with the present
> century. . . . All the more subtle workings both of the mind
> upon itself, and of external things upon the mind, escaped
> him; and no one, probably, who in a highly instructed age,
> ever attempted to give a rule to all human conduct, set out
> with a more limited knowledge either of the things by which
> human conduct *is,* or of those which it *should* be, influenced.
>
> This, then, is our idea of Bentham. He was a man both of
> remarkable endowments for philosophy, and of remarkable
> deficiencies for it: fitted, beyond almost any man, for drawing
> from his premises, conclusions not only correct, but whose
> general conception of human nature and life, furnished him
> with an unusally slender stock of premises. It is obvious what
> would be likely to be achieved by such a man; what a thinker,
> thus gifted and thus disqualified, could be in philosophy. He
> could be a systematic and accurately logical half-man; hunt-
> ing half-truths to their consequences and practical applica-
> tions, on a scale both of greatness and of minuteness not
> previously exemplified: and this is the character which pos-
> terity will probably assign to Bentham. (104–5)

I believe that Mill is displacing onto Bentham his secret opinions
about his father. Mill is recognizing that Bentham and "the late Mr.
Mill's" principal failure was that they could not cherish or even care.
He is recognizing that this rudimentary "meanness" and "barren-
ness" made the great Utilitarians "half-men." Mill has discovered

that his "precursors" identified one disease; but that they themselves fell victim to another. They contracted, he has realized, the disorder of incompleteness. They became afflicted with the pathology of indifference.

In "Civilization," Mill expresses the profoundness of his desire to discriminate himself from his father. In "Bentham," Mill begins to define the specific terms of his individualism. He begins to identify the specific respects in which he himself and the community of other people might recognize him as being a different, a "deeper," and a significantly better man than his father: a man more "fitted" for feeling and for loving, and therefore a man more "fitted" for the making of philosophy and for the living of life.

The remarkable insights that evoked and shaped "Bentham" would have terrified Mill at any earlier period of his life. At any earlier period, Mill would have feared that to distinguish himself from his parent would cause him to forfeit his ability to love and his ability to be loved. As he wrote "Bentham," he seems at last to have understood that he could separate himself from his father without becoming forced to loathe or even really to leave him. As he composed the essay, Mill seems to have comprehended that he could simultaneously defer to and "reject" his parent. He seems to have realized that he could at the same moment sustain and achieve some independence from the basal relationship of his life.

Mill apparently felt at least partially conscious of these developments in his thinking. He concludes his account of his "precursors'" strengths and limitations by remarking:

> The truths which are not Bentham's, which his philosophy takes no account of, are many and important; but his non-recognition of them does not put them out of existence; they are still with us, and it is a comparatively easy task that is reserved for us, to harmonize these truths with his. . . . Almost all rich veins of original and striking speculation have been opened by systematic half-minds: though whether these new thoughts drive out others as good, or are peacefully superadded to them, depends upon whether these half-minds are or are not followed in the same track by complete minds. The field of man's nature and life cannot be too much worked,

or in too many directions; until every clod is turned up the
work is imperfect; no whole truth is possible but by combin-
ing the points of view of all the fractional truths. (105–6)

Mill clearly is assigning paramountly to himself this high and holy
task of unification.[16] He is suggesting that he will individualize his
own character by extending and completing the psychology of his
father's generation. He is announcing that he will define his own
mind by "harmonizing" his mentors' "half-minds" with "all the
fractional truths" that have been created by other, equally incomplete interpreters of "man's nature and life."

To repair his parent's "non-recognitions"; to make the "half-man"
whole; to merge with his father even as he identified himself as
being heroically individual: all this was for Mill an almost complete
satiation, a nearly perfect fulfillment of his defining impulses. Always before Mill's radical ambivalence toward the utilitarian sensibility and toward the parent who had imposed that sensibility
upon him had frightened and frozen his imagination. In "Bentham," Mill discovered how to make his ambivalence work for him.
He discovered that his ambivalence was appropriate. He discovered
that his ambivalence offered him a principle of relation with the
Benthamic "character" at the same moment that it provided him
with a means by which to dissociate himself from that "character's"
deficiencies.

Mill seems to have realized how significant a discovery this was.
He seems to have recognized that he had achieved in "Bentham" a
reconciliation with the past and a principle of hope and power for
the future. With barely suppressed delight, he comments: "All great
movements, except revolutionary ones, are headed, not by those
who originate them, but by those who know best how to compromise between the old opinions and the new" (88). The thrusts of his
meaning are direct and clear. Mill is acknowledging that Jeremy
Bentham and "the late Mr. Mill" have died. He is suggesting that
his father and Bentham, the great and dominating "originators,"
were "half-men." He is identifying himself as a person who is both a
loyal son and an authentic adult. He is asserting that it will be his
unique and defining mission to complete his "precursors'" incomplete mentalities. And he is declaring that as he perfects his masters'
"nature and life" he will become the new head of Bentham's and

James Mill's "movement," the central figure in their symbiotic association with one another, and a free, whole, vigorously healthy, extremely powerful man.

In "Bentham," Mill induces himself to accept "the field" of his past and "the vein" of his future. In this remarkable essay, he allows himself to adore his father; but he forces himself to recognize and to separate himself from his father's "deficiency of Imagination." This was an entirely appropriate and a supremely healthy achievement. A man who has attained his thirty-second year well ought to bring his consciousness into peaceful and progressive order. That Mill could stimulate himself in 1838 to produce an equally conservative and "subversive" order and that he could create so loyal and yet so independent a recognition of Bentham's and his father's "nature and life" is an indication of how strong Mill's psychology essentially was.

"Bentham" is not only an authoritative criticism of the minds and the philosophies of Jeremy Bentham and James Mill. It is also a profoundly insightful study of the mentality and the purposes of John Mill. We should read "Bentham," I believe, as a curious and a wonderful version of the Pygmalion myth: a version in which an unwholesomely dependent vassal discerns and accepts his subordination, and yet incites himself to demand a considerable measure of autonomy, authenticity, and pleasure. Another prolegomenon to the *Autobiography*, "Bentham" proposes itself as a most significant document—as, indeed, virtually an entire stage—in the history of Mill's intellectual and imaginative development.

In 1840, Mill published "Coleridge," a companion piece to "Bentham." Like "Bentham," "Coleridge" addresses itself to a specific and a seemingly impersonal subject: the philosophy, the psychology, and the influence of Samuel Taylor Coleridge. However, "Coleridge," like "Bentham," also has subliminal energies and intentions. It expresses and explores Mill's personal interests and emotions. In "Coleridge" Mill completes the process of separation and integration he began in "The Spirit of the Age," "Civilization," and "Bentham." In this stunningly intelligent essay Mill powerfully advances his ambivalent rebellion against his parent and his past; and he at last commences his historic work as a moderate and libertarian subversive.

As he opens the essay, Mill makes it clear that he regards Coleridge as a heroic figure not only because of his individual merits but also, and perhaps primarily, because of his oppositeness from Bentham and James Mill. Mill begins his discussion by declaring that Coleridge was Bentham's equal in genius and in historical importance; but that he was "a man who saw so much farther into the complexities of the human intellect and feelings." [17] He observes that Coleridge greatly expanded Bentham's and his father's "short and easy method of referring all to the selfish interests of aristocracies, or priests, or lawyers, or some other species of imposters" (133). With considerable excitement he notes that, like himself but unlike Bentham and James Mill, Coleridge "looked upon the culture of the inward man as the problem of problems" (158). Throughout the essay Mill celebrates Coleridge as a rational poet. He lauds Coleridge as an artist who tried to create a thoroughly logical means by which to experience and to order illogical thoughts and sensations.

Mill does not suggest that he concurs with many of Coleridge's specific beliefs. He dissociates himself from almost all of Coleridge's opinions and programmes. Mill praises his subject as a spirit rather than as a practical philosopher. He argues that we should admire Coleridge's methods and points of view rather than, necessarily, his convictions and conclusions.

The language in which Mill introduces this complicated and characteristic theme is unconsciously expressive. He writes:

> Now the Germano-Coleridgean doctrine is, in our view of the matter, the result of . . . a re-action. It expressed the revolt of the human mind against the philosophy of the eighteenth century. It is ontological, because that was experimental; conservative because that was innovative; religious, because so much of that was infidel; concrete and historical, because that was abstract and metaphysical; poetical, because that was matter-of-fact and prosaic. (139)

Mill is careful to dissent from Coleridge's analyses and conclusions. But he praises Coleridge's methodologies, and he lauds the desires that inspired his work. [18] In another highly suggestive passage, Mill declares:

> Although we think the doctrines of Coleridge and the Germans, in the pure science of mind, erroneous, and have no

taste for their particular terminology, we are far from thinking that even in respect of this, the least valuable part of their
intellectual exertions, these philosophers have lived in vain.
The doctrines of the school of Locke stood in need of an entire renovation. . . . That men should begin by sweeping
this away from them was the first sign, that the age of real
psychology was about to commence. (144–45)

The significant phrase here is "the age of real psychology." Mill is
interested in Coleridge as a psychologist. More particularly, he is interested in Coleridge as a philosopher-poet who developed the science of psychology from its, as Mill believes, extremely problematic
origins in the work of Locke, Reid, Stewart, Brown, Priestley, and
Hartley. Still more particularly, Mill is interested in Coleridge as a
scientist and a prophet who guided the men of his generation in
their efforts to improve upon "the greatest accession to abstract psychology since Hartley, the 'Analysis of Pure Mind,' by the late Mr.
Mill" (145n.).

Mill is indicating that he found Coleridge a commanding figure
because Coleridge provided him with an attitude and with a specific
philosophical method upon which he could base his dissent from his
father's and Bentham's doctrines. Coleridge never convinced Mill
to adopt his terminologies, his positions, or his views. But he did
teach Mill to believe in the necessity to produce "an entire renovation" in the inherited philosophy and in the received styles of contemporary English culture. In this suggestion Coleridge gave Mill a
means by which he might objectify his personal "reaction" against
the philosophy of the eighteenth century. He gave Mill a means by
which he might justify his lifelong yearning to create a more "on-
tological," "religious," "concrete," "historical," and "poetical" experience than that which had been imposed upon him by Jeremy
Bentham and "the late Mr. Mill."

In this connection, it was especially important to Mill that Coleridge's writings provided him with a means by which to displace,
and thus to deny, the primal significance of his personal rebellion
against the Utilitarians. Mill suggests that one of the major reasons
that Coleridge's work was so attractive to him was because it described the philosophical and psychical materials against which they
both were reacting as a generational phenomenon. Coleridge de-

scribed Locke's and the Utilitarians' "infidel" persuasions as an impersonal historical development. Coleridge represented everything that was bleak and impious in James Mill's way of thinking as a neutral evolution, the creation not of one or of another individual person but of a whole "abstract and metaphysical" era in civilization. As he read Coleridge's literature, Mill found that to join with "the Germano-Coleridgean doctines" was to free himself from having to enter into formal and individualized conflict with "the late Mr. Mill." To join with Coleridge was to participate in a broadly based, completely dispassionate, conspicuously modern attempt to reaffirm and to reanimate the "science of mind" and the experiences of mind.

One of the principal reasons that he considered Coleridge to be such a compelling figure, Mill implies, was that he served as a kind of deflector. Coleridge supplied Mill with a methodology by which he could fulfill his irresistible need to "renovate" his existence without having explicitly to violate his sacrosanct relationship with his deceased but still deeply loved parent. Coleridge suggested, in short, that Mill himself might now enter into an "age of real psychology." Mill himself might now evolve into and behave as an independent man, while forever preserving the feelings of love and of loyalty that his childhood had implanted onto him.

There was another reason why Mill felt so attracted to Coleridge's philosophy. The "renovation" Mill wanted to create was as conservative as it was radical. He longed simultaneously to change and to perpetuate his inherited perceptions, principles, and pieties. Coleridge seemed to Mill to share this impulse. Indeed, Coleridge seemed to him to be the genius of this seemingly contradictory mentality. Mill celebrates his subject as a man who conducted "a revolution in opinion" (146) from protective or from essentially Tory grounds of thought and emotion. In an important and well-known passage, Mill declares:

> [Coleridge] has been the great awakener in this country of the spirit of philosophy, within the bounds of traditional opinions. . . . By Bentham, beyond all others, men have been led to ask themselves, in regard to any ancient or received opinion, Is it true? and by Coleridge, What is the meaning of it. (132–33).

The particular virtue of Coleridge, Mill is arguing, is that he demonstrated the uses of and the justifications for intelligent conservatism. He showed "the historic value of much which had ceased to be useful, [and] saw that institutions and creeds, now effete, had rendered essential service to civilization, and still filled a place in the human mind, and in the arrangements of society, which could not without utmost peril be left vacant" (155). Coleridge saw "in many of the institutions most cankered with abuse, necessary elements of civilized society, though in a form and vesture no longer suited to the age" (155). Coleridge "thus produced," Mill contends, "not a piece of party advocacy, but a philosophy of society, in the only form which it is yet possible, that of a philosophy of history; not a defense of particular ethical or religious doctrines, but a contribution, the largest made by any class of thinkers, toward the philosophy of human culture (156).[19] Mill concludes:

> In the details of Coleridge's political opinions there is much
> good, and much that is questionable or worse. . . . [But] he
> has helped to bring forward great principles, either implied
> in the old English institutions, or at least opposed to the new
> tendencies. (176–77)

Mill views Coleridge as a great preserver. At the same time, he regards Coleridge as a great subversive. He understands him as a philosopher who, like Bentham, required all institutions and all beliefs to subject themselves to ongoing reexamination and careful revision.
It is here that Coleridge was most exciting and most valuable to Mill. Coleridge seemed to serve as a standing example of the necessity both to do away with "abuse" and to protect order; the necessity both to repudiate everything devitalizing in contemporary thought and life, and to preserve the "necessary elements of civilized society." Mill clearly conceived that Coleridge's uses in this respect were at once social and individual. As in "Civilization," Mill imagined in "Coleridge" that the various institutions, structures, and forces of "civilized society" affect equally the culture of the polity and culture of the self. Just as a people living in a community must practice "habitual submission to law and government" (149), an individ-

ual—Mill himself—must experience love and obedience to a parent. Love and obedience, however, may need to be reconsidered and revised. Love and obedience, like all other "traditional" modes of being, may need to be made more "suited" in "form and vesture" to "the age"—to the changing requirements of historical time and to the changing requirements of an individual as he becomes an adult.

From Coleridge, Mill learned that the "institutions and creeds, now effete, [which] still filled a place" in his own "human mind" could be reinterpreted and reinvigorated, rather than with "the utmost peril" be forced to become merely "vacant." In Coleridge, Mill found a prophet and a practicing proponent of his own deepest psychological aspirations. He found a man of genius who could validate his impulse to achieve a seemingly impossible act: the creation of liberty and of health within the context and the rewards of a continuing "submission" to his "old tendencies."

Throughout the essay Mill speaks of Coleridge as the embodiment or the exemplar of this complicated synthesis. He repeatedly refers to Coleridge as both the Utilitarians' opposite and their spiritual associate. He continually suggests that Coleridge diametrically differed from Bentham and "the late Mr. Mill"; but that their differences and seeming hostility toward one another did not constitute an antagonism so much as a complex completeness or totality. "It would be difficult," Mill declares, "to find two persons of philosophic eminence more exactly the contrary of one another" (134). And yet, he continues:

> Contraries, as logicians say, are but . . . the things which are
> farthest from one another *in the same kind.* The two men
> agreed in being the men who in their age and country, did
> most to enforce, by precept and example, the necessity of a
> philosophy. . . . They employed, indeed, for the most part,
> different materials; but as the materials of both were real ob-
> servations, the genuine product of experience—the results
> will in the end be found not hostile, but supplementary, to
> one another. Of their methods of philosophizing the same
> thing may be said: they were different, yet both were legiti-
> mate logical processes. In every respect the two men are each
> other's 'complementing counterpart.' (134–35)

Mill is contending that all the apparently absolute divergences in the two schools' values, opinions, and methods in fact represent an intricate convergence. Properly regarded, he maintains, all the seeming conflicts between Bentham and Coleridge may be recognized as concealed affinities. All the quarrels and disputations between Coleridge and "the late Mr. Mill" may be understood as symptoms of a hidden mutuality of experience and of purpose; a disguised but an essential congruence of passionate and sincere, completely admirable involvement with systematic rational thought.

Throughout "Coleridge," Mill proposes that in both philosophy and life the great principle of truth lies in communion rather than in conflict. He also proposes that in both philosophy and life the most unusual and yet the most important purpose of mind is to perceive unity and to effect reconciliation. These themes and his power to articulate them seem to have deeply excited Mill. In a mood of intense subconscious arousal, he exclaims:

> All students of man and society who possess that first requisite for so difficult a study, a due sense of its difficulties, are aware that the besetting danger is not so much of embracing falsehood for truth, as of mistaking part of the truth for the whole. It might be plausibly maintained that in every one of the leading controversies, past or present, in social philosophy, both sides were in the right in what they affirmed, though wrong in what they denied; and that if either could have been made to take the other's views in addition to its own, little more would have been needed to make its doctrine perfect. (136–37)

He continues:

> The history of opinion is generally an oscillation between [extremes]. . . . Every excess in either direction determines a corresponding re-action; improvement consisting only in this, that the oscillation, each time, departs rather less widely from the centre, and an every-increasing tendency is manifested to settle finally in it. (138–39)

Here, as throughout the essay, Mill rejects the very idea of antagonism. He refuses to believe in either incompatability or hostility. He asserts that clashes and contradictions reflect only ignorance or misunderstanding. He insists that oppositions and collisions always can be avoided or reconciled. He imagines that all life can be made to become a process of gradual convergence into harmonious accord.

Mill never recommends tepidity or torpor. He never suggests that any person ever should equivocate. He repeatedly contends that one must advance one's persuasions and one's convictions as ardently as possible. He feels certain that "improvement" can occur only if the "oscillation" of individuals' opinions are, at least initially, extreme. In "Coleridge," as throughout his literature, Mill argues, wonderfully, for passionate intensity in philosophy and in life. He demands that we contest for our visions and our views. He demands that we repudiate every idea and every action that seems to ourself invidious or vicious. The point, Mill proclaims, is not to shrink from struggle. The point is to comprehend that all struggles are transitional. The point is to understand that all disputations are primitive and preludial. In "Coleridge," Mill argues that conflict is premoral. He believes that in both civic and individual existence there always exists a calm and beautiful "centre," which we eventually may find and which we eventually may embrace.

In each of his remarks about Coleridge and conservatism, philosophy and religion, thought and feeling, Mill subconsciously was identifying and legitimizing the nature and the requirements of his own imagination. As he wrote the essay, Mill was attempting to transform his strongest demands and drives into a theory of history and an organized ethos. If we read "Coleridge" carefully, we can observe Mill at the very moment in which he discovers that he is a man who reverences and who longs to share Coleridge's feelings of catholicity, coherence, and calm. We can observe Mill at the very moment in which he realizes that, like Coleridge, he is a person who needs to make logic cohere with love; and who yearns to make love cohere with independence, creativity, and continuity. As we read "Coleridge," we encounter Mill commanding himself to believe in and to act at the behest of his own seemingly contradictory character. We hear him directing himself to recognize and to accept his own simultaneously radical and conservative consciousness. We observe him equipping himself to undertake his own historical, generational, and supremely individualistic work.

As he composed "Coleridge," Mill concluded that finding and promulgating "the centre" constitutes the fundamental metaphysical activity of man. His major subliminal purpose in writing the essay seems to have been to enlist himself in this activity. Certainly Mill attempts in "Coleridge" to claim for himself the principal role in defining that core of validity and vitality that had been approached but finally missed or exceeded by Coleridge, Bentham, and "the late Mr. Mill." With extreme excitement, he declares:

> The limited philosophical public of this country is as yet too exclusively divided between those to whom Coleridge and the views which he promulgated or defended are *all,* and those to whom they are *nothing.* A great thinker can only be justly estimated when his thoughts have worked their way into minds formed in a different school; have been wrought and moulded into consistency with all other true and relevant thoughts; when the noisy conflict of half-truths, angrily denying one another, has subsided, and ideas which seemed mutually incompatible, have been found only to require mutual limitation. This time has not yet come for Coleridge. The spirit of philosophy in England, like that of religion, is still rootedly sectarian. (135–36)

Mill is defining himself here as the one man in England who is most qualified by education and by temperament to synthesize the seemingly "incompatible" opinions and methods of the Utilitarians and the Coleridgeans. To discern a single, harmonious totality within his mentors' many angry and incomplete "half-truths," to identify and personally to occupy a single, peaceful "centre" within the chaotic and bellicose "oscillations" of his country's greatest philosophers, seemed to Mill in 1840 to be uniquely his own possibility and mission.

Mill makes no effort to conceal the importance he placed upon this enterprise. He declares: "Whoever could master the premises and combine the methods of both [the Utilitarians and the Coleridgeans], would possess the entire English philosophy of his age"

(135). The words "master" and "possess" may seem curious and perhaps even unpleasant in this context. They connote ownership and might. They imply that Mill believed he could acquire independence and legitimacy from his work of "combination." They also imply that he believed he could acquire public eminence, and even some degree of authority over other persons' minds. As he wrote "Coleridge," Mill seems subconsciously to have been seeking and subconsciously expecting to achieve not only personal fulfillment but also a kind of social power.

We may understand how he came to think and to feel in this way. I have been suggesting that for Mill the issues and the stakes which were involved in his discourse were both social and characterological. To unite Bentham's and his father's love of logic with Coleridge's love of loving; to merge Bentham's and his parent's glorification of objectivity with Coleridge's celebration of feeling; to connect Bentham's and "the late Mr. Mill's" subversiveness with Coleridge's conservatism; above all, to domesticate or to deny his own conflicts and antagonisms: all this, for Mill, should be to achieve resolution, completeness, and relative serenity in his personal imagination. To effect a synthesis and a general truth in the social philosophy of Europe should be to produce an absolute integration in Mill's own intelligence. I believe Mill speaks of and about power in "Coleridge" because he subliminally realized that he was confronting his own consciousness in the essay. He knew, I believe, that by writing about his forebears he was engaging and satisfying his previously beleaguered sensibility in a new and a most promising manner.

If we examine closely the language in which Mill describes his ideas about the nature of "the centre," we can see that he intuitively understood the personal implications of his work in "Coleridge." Mill remarks, we recall, that "contraries" are but "the things which are farthest from one another *in the same kind.*" He suggests that various "methods of philosophizing" may be "different, yet both legitimate logical processes." Men who disagree with one another "will in the end be found," he declares, "not hostile, but supplementary to one another." Regarded in the proper light, he asserts, philosophers who do not accord or concur with one another ultimately may be recognized as "each other's 'complementing counterpart.'" As we reconsider the meanings of these passages, we realize that Mill has produced the perfect definition of a healthy individuation. He has created, we realize, the best possible description of a necessary and a normative experience of filiation. Difference within sameness. Uniqueness within kinship and kindredness. Conflict within compatibility and love. Novelty within continuity. In "Coleridge," Mill is announcing to himself, to his deceased father, and to the world at large that he at last has found it posssible to achieve identification. He is announcing that he will accomplish selfhood; but that he will retain and incorporate the passions and the prerogatives of sonship. He is declaring that he and his father are two "different" persons, "not hostile, but supplementary, to one another." He is stating, firmly and cleanly, that he and his parent are "contraries," but *"in the same kind"*; they are "in every respect . . . each other's 'complementing counterpart.'"

This was for Mill a cathartic and an extraordinarily liberating achievement. In the act of imagining and writing "Coleridge," Mill finally freed his lifelong yearning to establish and to accept himself. In the course of describing his responses to Coleridge, Bentham, and "the late Mr. Mill," Mill defined a response to his own history and character. He developed his chronic and previously paralyzing ambivalences into a coherent consciousness and a creed. He converted his constitutional conflicts into the basis of a formal philosophy and an organized personality. "Coleridge" marks the end of a phase in Mill's development. The essay presents itself as the last of Mill's infantile, reactive pieces; and as the first of his mature, fully creative works. From this point, from this "centre," Mill felt himself "fitted" to undertake his purely personal, purely independent, purely inventive acts of imagination. When we read "Coleridge," we encounter a person who is banishing terror and embracing power. We encounter a man who is exorcising dependence and seizing sovereignty. We encounter, it is not too much to say, a major artist who is repudiating disorder and claiming health, happiness, hope, and his own genius.

—————————————3

Love and Marriage

During the 1830s Mill gradually allowed himself to experience another kind of maturation. In 1830 W. J. Fox introduced him to Harriet Hardy Taylor, the wife of a prosperous London merchant. Harriet was beautiful, brilliantly gifted, deeply curious, and anything but content with her condition as a bourgeois wife and mother. She felt intrigued with Mill; and he with her. Between 1830 and 1832 they met frequently. Their friendship never became overtly sexual. But their experience of one another was erotic in everything other than the actually physical sense. By 1832 Harriet felt impelled to inform her husband about the state of her feelings. John Taylor initially pressed Harriet to renounce her love for Mill. She tried to comply with her husband's wishes, but she could not. An extraordinarily generous man, John Taylor agreed to tolerate the affair. Throughout the 1830s and 1840s, Mill and Harriet met and even traveled together with great frequency. Their intimacy was absolute. But their emotions and the fact itself of their relationship had to be concealed from the world. Mill and Harriet suffered gravely from the restrictions and from the hypocrisies to

88

which they were forced to submit themselves. Their love for one another was ardent, however, and they made their life together as close and as comforting as their circumstances permitted it to be. For many years Harriet and Mill lived almost as man and wife. At last, in July 1849, John Taylor died. For two years after his death, the lovers uncomfortably observed the proprieties of mourning. In the spring of 1851, they quietly married.[1]

The love affair of John Mill and Harriet Taylor makes one of the most peculiar and one of the most engaging relationships of the nineteenth century. Generations of readers have felt intrigued and delighted by the intensity and the Platonism of the lovers' devotion to one another. The constancy and the sweetness of the Mills' long courtship and marriage, the intimacy and the trust of their interaction, seem strange and wonderful. Equally strange and wonderful is the matter of Mill's seemingly miraculous resilience. We wonder how Mill could have loved anyone. Certainly it is suprising that he could have loved anyone other than his father. And that he could have loved so earnestly and so fervently! That he could have loved so happily! We cannot help but feel mystified and interested. We cannot help but wonder how Mill perceived Harriet; and how he developed and released his passion for her.

Mill reveals a great deal about his attitudes toward Harriet and toward the experience of loving her in a letter which he wrote in 1850. "Your impromptu words," he comments, "almost always are . . . a hundred times better than any I could find by study." He goes on to declare:

> What a perfect orator you would make—& what changes
> might be made in the world by such a one, with such oppor-
> tunities as thousands of male dunces have. But you are to me,
> & would be to anyone who knew you, the type of Intellect—
> because you have all the faculties in equal perfection—you
> can both think & impress the thought on others—& can
> both judge what ought to be done, & do it. As for me,
> nothing but the division of labour would make me
> useful. . . . I am but fit to be one wheel in an engine not to
> be the self moving engine itself—a real majestic intellect,
> not to say moral nature, like yours, I can only look up to &
> admire—but while you can love me as you so sweetly & so

beautifully shewed in that hour yesterday, I have all I care for
or desire for myself—& wish for nothing except not to disap-
point you—& to be so happy as to be some good to you (who
are all good to me) before I die.[2]

Mill repeatedly expressed his conviction that his lover was almost
preternaturally intelligent and compassionate, and that he himself
was "but fit" to assist and to interpret her. He thought of Harriet,
he once told her, as "the profoundest thinker & most consummate
reasoner [I] ever have known.[3] Harriet was, he wrote to F. J. Furnivall, "the noblest and wisest being I ever have known.[4] On another occasion he remarked: "All that excites admiration when found
separately in others, seemed brought together in her."[5] Mill did not
shrink from publicly proclaiming these views. In the *Autobiography*
he declares: "The friendship [with Harriet] has been the honour and
the chief blessing of my existence, as well as the source of all that I
have attempted to do, or hope to effect hereafter, for human improvement" (*Autobiography*, 111). He continues:

> [She] could not receive an impression or an experience with-
> out making it the source or the occasion of an accession of
> wisdom. . . . Alike in the highest regions of speculation and
> in the smallest practical concerns of life, her mind was the
> same perfect instrument; always seizing the essential idea or
> principle. . . . Her intellectual gifts did but minister to a
> moral character at once the noblest and the best balanced
> which I have ever met with in life.[6] (*Autobiography*, 112–13)

As we read these passages, it may seem to us that we have heard
Mill speak in this way before. The passages sound, we realize, like a
host of similarly excited passages which Mill earlier had written
about his father. Mill seems subconsciously to have understood this.
At one point in the *Autobiography* he makes the parallelism in his
excitements explicit and thematic. He comments: "In the power of
influencing by mere force of mind and character, the convictions and
purposes of others, . . . [my father] left, as far as my knowledge
extends, no equal among men, and but one among women" (*Autobiography*, 123). This anything but casual remark strongly suggests
that Mill's love for his wife occurred as a variation upon his love for

his parent. Mill is indicating that throughout his life, in his "knowledge," there have been two persons who have exercised a decisive "power of influencing" him: his omnipotent parent and his "perfect" wife.

The possibility that there might have been a close association between his conception of his father and his conception of his lover evidently did not disturb Mill. This seems to have been an association or an identification which he actively sought. In one of his most suggestive letters, he asks:

> *Is* there really any distinction between the highest masculine and the highest feminine character? I do not mean the mechanical *acquirements*; those, of course, will very commonly be different. But the women, of all I have known, who possessed the highest measure of what are considered feminine qualities, have combined with them more of the highest *masculine* qualities than I have ever seen in but one or two men and those one or two men were also in many respects almost women. I suspect it is the second-rate people of the two sexes that are unlike, the first-rate are alike.[7]

Mill has made a complicated declaration. He is asserting that the "highest" male and the "highest" female characters are in every important respect coessential. He is contending that "first-rate" intellectual and moral "qualities" always "make [a] character" which is beyond gender. He is trying to persuade himself that none of the "distinctions"—and none of the threats—of sexual differentiation need be acknowledged between people who live "in the highest regions of speculation." This is Mill's ultimate act of synthesis. He is attempting to "harmonize" not simply differences of opinion and differences of philosophical method. He is trying to "combine" differences of physiology and differences of gender identity.

There was something enormous at stake for Mill in this identification. His fanciful confusion about "the distinction between" the masculine and the feminine, his ingenious conceit that persons such as Harriet and James were fundamentally "alike," seems to have become the mechanism by which Mill completed his resolution of his protracted and enervating Oedipus crisis. By discovering and by loving a woman whom he could regard as "the highest feminine character," Mill found a way, it appears, to transfer almost all his hysterical libidinal excitement away from his father and onto a more receptive and a more socially acceptable figure. By consciously de-sexualizing both Harriet and James, he evidently could feel uncon-scious excitement without having to recognize the nature of his ex-citement: without having to recognize, specifically, that his excite-ment was erotic, and that his eroticism was directed toward his parent.

I am suggesting that by loving Harriet, Mill at last managed to unite himself with his father; but to do so in a safe, structured, un-assailable, and completely sublimated or symbolic manner. I believe that he reacted so powerfully to Harriet because he subconsciously regarded her as "the noblest and best balanced" version of James "whom he ever met with in life." Because he thought of her as a surrogate for his father, Mill could think of loving Harriet as "the noblest and best balanced" version of arousal and fulfillment that he ever had been able to experience. In loving Harriet, Mill was loving not only a licit woman but an illicit image. He was both reacting to a person and discharging a compulsion. Earlier I discussed the means by which Mill liberated his conscious intelligence. Here I believe we may discern the means by which he freed his subconscious intelli-gence. We may see that Mill relieved the irreducible demands of his inverse Oedipal neurosis by devising a socially unobjectionable and personally very stimulating substitute for the object of his obsessive admiration and passion.

Certainly Mill transferred onto his wife his father's principal func-tions and roles. His descriptions of their relationship make it clear that he regarded Harriet as a prophet and a teacher whose insights and energies might rescue him from his own ignorance and unnatu-ralness. In the *Autobiography*, for example, Mill declares:

To be admitted into any great degree of mental intercourse with a being of [her] qualities, could not help but have a most beneficial influence on my development. . . . What I owe, even intellectually, to her, is, in its detail, almost in-finite. (*Autobiography*, 113)

Later he comments: "The properly human element [in my work] came from her: in all that concerned the application of philosophy to the exigencies of human society and progess, I was her pupil" (*Auto-biography*, 149). In his diary, Mill wrote: "Bitterly do I feel how little I have yet done as the interpreter of one whose intellect is as much profounder than mine as her heart is nobler."[8] Later he remarked:

> Whenever I look back at any of my own writings of two or three years previous, they seem to me like the writings of some stranger whom I have known long ago. I wish that my acquisition of power to do better had kept pace with the continual education of my standing point and change of bear-ings towards all the great subjects of thought. But the expla-nation is that I owe the enlargement of my ideas and feelings to *her* influence, and that she could not in the same degree give me powers of execution.[9]

Mill submitted himself to his wife's tutelage not only in "all the great subjects of thought" but also in all the merely mundane affairs of his daily life. Harriet managed Mill's household, transacted with his tradesmen, and paid his bills. She apparently even edited his social correspondence. In 1853, for example, Mill wrote: "[I] have had a note from Adderley which I enclose with the answer I propose sending when dearest one has made it right."[10] His dependence evi-dently was unbounded. He deferred to Harriet's opinions and judg-ments in his most casual and in his most important decisions. After his mother's death, to cite but one instance, he declared: "I do not think we ought to take [my mother's legacy]—what do you think? . . . I have a very strong feeling about it."[11] Eight days later he re-marked : "About that matter of my mother's inheritance, of course as your feeling is so directly contrary, mine is wrong, & I give it up entirely."[12] In all things, Mill told his wife, he "never should long continue of an opinion different from yours on a subject which you have fully considered."[13] About all questions great and small he begged that "you dearest one will tell me what your perfect judge-ment & your feeling decide."[14] He went so far as to exclaim: "I should like every one to know that I am the Dumont & you the originating mind, the Bentham, bless her."[15]

The conception of himself as an incapable and subservient "pupil" apparently was necessary for Mill. It seems that he could live and that he could love only by entering into an abject social and psychosexual situation. He evidently could experience communion and affection only by deprecating himself and glorifying somebody else. This carefully orchestrated combination of abasement and aggrandizement appears to have served a complex and crucial function. It seems that from Harriet, as earlier from his father, Mill hoped to receive not only wisdom and truth but also validation and acceptance. From his partner, as earlier from his parent, he needed to absorb the certainty, the correctness, and the contentment that he associated with "a real majestic intellect." As a lover Mill appears to have felt and to have acted much as he had done as a son. In his adulthood as in his youth, he made love in order to achieve identification. He made love in order to secure, if only by projection, something more coherent and more satisfying than his own chronic consciousness of confusion and imperfection.

Mill was able to discern one intensely gratifying difference between Harriet and his father. Throughout the *Autobiography* he eulogizes his wife as a person who was incapable of behaving in his father's coercive and co-optative way. He repeatedly celebrates Harriet as a woman whose leading characteristic was her great and gratuitous tenderness. He declares, for example: "The passion for justice might have been thought to be her strongest feeling, but for her boundless generosity, and a lovingness ever ready to pour itself forth on any or all human beings who were capable of giving the smallest feeling in return" (*Autobiography*, 113).

As we have seen, neither "lovingness" nor "return" were prominent elements of Mill's earlier experience of love. He responded fervently to his wife's ideal, as it were antipaternal gentleness. With joy and abandon Mill gave Harriet his entire, long-suppressed capacity for "feeling." Significantly, his letters to Harriet frequently seem to express gratitude as well as exultation. Mill adored and rejoiced in Harriet, it often appears, not only because of what he felt for her but also—and perhaps primarily—because she allowed him to feel. The locutions with which Mill closes his love letters are particularly expressive. He concludes one letter with the phrase: "Addieu, delight of my life.[16] He ends another: "Addieu con tutti gli amori et baci possibili."[17] On other occasions he exclaims: "Addio con tutti i baci possibili—ah dearest how I do love you." "Good night my dearest dearest love—I kiss her mentally with my whole heart." "Addio mia divinia —mia addorata."[18] Mill's eagerness and enthusiasm press against the confines of language. He draws upon English, French, and Italian indiscriminately, as though he feels driven to explore the entire human word stock in his effort to produce a continually fresh vocabularly by which to communicate and to preserve his feelings of arousal and delight. In all his letters to Harriet, Mill seems to chuckle or to chortle. We almost can hear him thinking: I can love. I do love. Day after day, I love and I love and I love. And what is more, what is the wonder of wonders, I am loved in return.

It appears that from his experience with Harriet, Mill derived not only satisfaction and pleasure but also a conscious awareness of his own selfhood. It was like him to attribute his heightened sense of individuality not to the development of his own energies and capacities, but to the "boundless generosity" and vitality of his lover. In 1849 he told Harriet: "When I left you my darling . . . I was full of life & animation & vigour of wish and purpose, because I was fresh from the immediate influence of your blessed presence." [19] In a later, most remarkable letter, Mill makes it clear that he felt indebted to his wife for more than his new feelings of "animation & vigour." He believed, it seems, that he had received his sheer, elemental humanness from Harriet. Mill writes:

> My own precious darling wife what sweet words! what good
> it did & does me to read that one word—she knows which—
> the sweetest word she can say—when she can say or write
> that, I know she must be loving me & feeling all that it is
> happiest to think of & all that I most wish for. I needed it
> too, for words of love in absence are as they always were,
> what keeps the blood going in the veins—but for them
> whenever I am not anxious & triste a mourir for fear she
> should not be loving me, I should only have a sort of hyber-
> nating existence like those animals found in the inside of a
> rock. [20]

Loving Harriet appears to have become the mechanism by which Mill confronted and freed himself from the terrible specter of affectlessness. Anxiety, sadness, self-hatred, and, ultimately, despairing indifference always before had made the secret core of Mill's sensibility. The experience of love eventually came to seem to this abused, almost absolutely repressed man something like a divine gift. Recognition, acceptance, communion, and pleasure proposed themselves to Mill as unexpected and, as it were, unpredictable treasures: the offerings, it often seemed to him, of a sacred and an all-powerful, wonderfully beneficent deity.

The extent to which Mill felt spiritually and even biologically dependent upon Harriet is startling and touching. In 1854, while suffering from consumption, he recorded the following entry in his diary:

> What a sense of protection is given by the consciousness of
> being loved, and what an additional sense, over and above
> this, by being near the one by whom one is and wishes to be
> loved the best. I have experience at present of both these
> things; for I feel as if no really dangerous illness could actu-
> ally happen to me while I have her to care for me; and yet I
> feel as if by coming away from her I had parted from a kind
> of talisman, and was more open to the attacks of the enemy
> than while I was with her.[21]

Mill regarded his wife, it seems, as a celestial being—a benign and beatific angel of mercy. In fact he regarded his lover as a goddess. During the last year of Harriet's life, Mill raised this subconscious conceit into a conscious conviction. In one of his last letters to his "addorata" he exclaims:

> Reading this last letter through I find it all dry narrative
> without a word of the love I have been feeling & which is my
> comfort & strength. My darling will know that I am think-
> ing all the time of her & that her existence & love are to me
> what the Deity is to a devout person—I feel through every-
> thing that she is the fond of my existence, all the rest plays
> on the surface.[22]

From his earliest years Mill had longed to find a "Deity" power-ful, generous, and gentle enough to impart onto him all that his father had made him fear that he lacked: "life & animation & vigour of wish & purpose"; "a sense of protection"; "the consciousness of being loved"; "comfort & strength." In his wife he believed that he at last had discovered that exteriorized self—that "talisman" and "fond"—which his difficult parent had refused to become. Mill cherished Harriet because she was the first and the only person whom he had "ever met with in life" who was equipped and who was willing completely to accept and completely to govern his extraordinarily subordinative, extraordinarily tender sensibility.[23]

We do not know if the Mills ever physically consummated their passion for one another.[24] We do know that throughout their life together they both expressed strong reservations about the dignity and the appropriateness of carnal sexuality. In an early version of the *Autobiography*, for example, Mill remarks:

> We disdained, as every person not the slave of his animal
> appetites must do, the abject notion that the strongest and
> tenderest friendship cannot exist between a man and a
> woman without a sensual relation, or that any impulse of that
> lower character cannot be put aside when regard for the feel-
> ings of others, or even when only prudence and personal dig-
> nity require it. (*Early Draft*, 171)

Passionate emotions may be "put aside." But they must become discharged in some way. Earlier I suggested that for many years before he loved and lived with Harriet, Mill had displaced his "animal appetites" and his "sensual relations" onto his literature. In many of his letters and journal entries, Mill indicates that Harriet understood and shared this impulse. Not only, then, did Harriet allow Mill to liberate his libidinal "appetites." She also allowed him to express his "appetites" in the manner that he found most comfortable.

That the activities of thinking and writing became the idiom of the Mills' sexuality seems beyond doubt. In the *Autobiography*, Mill describes Harriet and himself as "two persons [who had] their thoughts and speculations entirely in common. . . ." He recalls that "not only during the years of [their] married life, but during many of the years of confidential friendship which preceded," their "daily life" consisted of "probing [to great] depths . . . all subjects of intellectual or moral interest." Their entire relationship proposed itself to him as a "partnership of thought, feeling, and writing." His own literature, Mill excitedly observes, was "not the work of one mind, but the fusion of two." Particularly *On Liberty* seemed to him a work that both emerged from and embodied "the conjunction of her mind with mine" (*Autobiography*, 145, 143, 114, 150).

Mill makes it apparent that he viewed this "fusion" or "conjunction" as a sensual union: as, indeed, a kind of passionate and permanent intercourse. He seems to have regarded the very texts of their letters to one another as libidinal surfaces. He often commented, for example, upon the erotic materiality of Harriet's calligraphy. In 1854 he wrote: "I shall get her beautiful writing tomorrow which is the next (though far removed) to her beautiful self."[25] In 1858 he declared: "Every word of her handwriting is so precious & so delightful."[26] On other occasions Mill was even more explicit about his sense that their letters to one another were an important manifestation of their sexuality. He closes one of his most striking communications of this kind by asking: "Will my darling kiss her next letter just in the middle of the first line of writing—the kiss will come safe & I shall savourer it."[27] About "the lines of writing" that he and Harriet addressed to the general public Mill was more discreet but hardly less excited. He once referred to the *System of Logic* as "my mental offspring."[28] In 1853 he remarked:

> We must finish the best we have got to say, & not only that, but publish it while we are alive—I do not see what living depository there is likely to be of our thoughts, or who in this weak generation that is growing up will even be capable of thoroughly mastering & assimilating your ideas, much less of reoriginating them—so we must write & print them, & then they can wait until there are again thinkers.[29]

In 1854 he wrote:

> I have been feeling much . . . about the shortness & uncertainty of life & the wrongness of having so much of the best of what we have to say, so long unwritten & in the power of chance. . . . Two years, well employed, would enable us I think to get the most of it in a state fit for printing—if not in the best form for popular effect, yet in the state of concentrated thought—a sort of mental pemmican, which thinkers,

when there are any after us, may nourish themselves with &
then dilute for other people.[30]

Verbalizing their "thoughts" and "ideas" evidently seemed to the
Mills a satisfactory way of expressing their libidinal identities. They
appear to have regarded their literature and their letters as most
other lovers regard their sexuality: as the most complete and the
most exciting manifestation of their feelings about one another. The
letters I have cited lead us to an even more extreme conclusion.
Writing apparently proposed itself to both Harriet and Mill as a re-
generative activity. Whether defined as "mental offspring," "living
depository," or "mental pemmican," the discourse they created together seemed to these closely "conjoined" people to symbolize the
children whom they never had. Harriet and Mill both lived to work;
and they both seem to have conceived of their work as the elemental
stuff of their intellectual, moral, and erotic lives.

The erotic content of their literature and the libidinal structure of
their marriage seem to have become confirmed and secured by Harriet's willingness to assume control of Mill's career. We learn from his
correspondence that deferring to his wife's professional judgments
and decisions greatly relieved Mill's chronic self-doubts, and made
him feel both thankful and stimulated. *"I am not fit,"* he commented
in one letter, "to write on anything but the outskirts of the great
questions of feeling & life without you to prompt me as well as to
keep me right."[31] On another occasion he remarked: "I want my
angel to tell me what should be the next essay written. I have done
all I can for the subject she last gave me."[32] Some months later he
wrote:

> Perhaps my darling will suggest something—she may con-
> ceive but I am sure she does not know what a difference it
> makes in the possibility of any verve in writing on a subject
> & even in the capacity of writing about it at all, for it to have
> been of her suggesting.[33]

"What would be the use of my outliving you!" he cries. "I could
write nothing worth keeping alive except with your prompting."[34]
Mill seems to have believed that writing under his wife's supervi-

sion and direction brought Harriet and himself into a completely
unified state. His own skills, he thought, were sheerly composi-
tional. Harriet's, he imagined, were conceptual and inspirational.
Her "feeling & life" and his mechanical ability, her authority and his
submissiveness, her "verve" and his "capacity" appeared to Mill perfectly to cohere in his literature. He conceived that their disparate
talents and their separate natures coalesced into a single, abundantly
strong and fertile "character" each time that he wrote on "the great
questions of feeling & life."

Probably this situation so much delighted and inspired Mill because it satisfied the compulsions that always had dominated his
consciousness. We have learned that from his earliest years Mill had
yearned to become incorporated into another, more powerful person's
life. Particularly, we have learned, he had wanted his father to appropriate and to animate him. We have seen, too, that Mill longed to
become identified solely by his philosophies and his writings. We
have seen that he desperately wanted to reduce himself and all his
imaginative complexities to his rational intelligence and its works.
In his wife, Mill at last found a powerful person who would love
him; a person who would express her love by absorbing him into
herself; and a person who would encourage and assist him to displace
his instinctual drives onto his literature. In Harriet, it appears, Mill
at last found the presiding genius whom he always had needed and
whom he always unconsciously had sought: a gentle, wise, and
dominating father-substitute who could salvage his existence by
conferring shape, "capacity," and tender, reciprocal "feeling" upon
his taut and tormented intelligence.

Certainly his relationship with Harriet fulfilled Mill. It is not
possible to overstate the extent to which their union excited and satisfied him. We may derive some sense of Mill's commitment to the
marriage and to its symbolic meanings from a letter he wrote in
1852 to his sister Clara. In one of the very few avowedly angry communications that he ever allowed himself to make, Mill declared:
"You are entirely mistaken if you suppose that I said you had been
uncivil to my wife. I said that you have been wanting in all good
feeling and even common civility to *us*. My wife and I are one." [35]
Mill is defining here, succinctly and fiercely, the state of mind in
which he and his wife lived. He and Harriet were so compatible—
or so symbiotic—with one another that they believed themselves to

constitute something like a single personality.[36] This unity or duality seemed to Mill neither dangerous nor ridiculous. The idea of his "oneness" with his wife seems to have given him the first and perhaps the single complete gratification of his otherwise epically unhappy life.

I do not mean to suggest that the marriage and its contentments caused Mill to feel entirely or uncomplicatedly joyful. The very fact that his wife seemed to him "the only good of [his] life"[37] made him feel acutely vulnerable to her inevitable and harmless variations of manner and mood. In his correspondence Mill indicates that he became deeply wounded whenever he believed, rightly or wrongly, that Harriet felt dissatisfied with him. In 1855, for example, he wrote:

> Ah darling I had a horrible dream lately—I had come back to her & she was sweet & loving like herself at first, but presently she took a complete dislike to me saying that I was changed much for the worse—I am terribly afraid lest she should think so, not that I see any cause for it, but because I know how deficient I am in self consciousness & self observation, & how often when she sees me again after I have been even a short time abroad she is disappointed.[38]

Mill loved Harriet and he felt loved by her. But he never could thoroughly free himself from his painful consciousness of inadequacy and incompleteness. He never could feel himself entirely safe from other persons'—even from his wife's—"dislike," "disappointment," and disapproval.

The totality of his dependence exposed Mill to another kind of suffering. His need to regard his wife as the center of all existence intensified the marriage and excited his imagination. Often, though, his exaggerated idea of his wife's significance produced considerable and, so to speak, unnecessary trauma. In his diary for 1844, Mill recorded an entry which is characteristic in its suggestion of the gratuitous suffering which he manufactured for himself. He writes:

> If human life is governed by superior beings, how greatly must the power of evil intelligences surpass that of the good, when a soul and an intellect like hers, such as the good prin-

ciple perhaps never succeeded in creating before—one who seems intended for an inhabitant of some remote heaven, and who wants nothing but a position of power to make a heaven of even this stupid and wretched earth—when such a being *must* perish like all the rest of us in a few years, and *may* in a few months from a mere alteration in the structure of a few fibres or membranes, the exact parallels of which are found in every quadruped![39]

Harriet stimulated and fulfilled Mill. But his impulse to represent her as the nucleus and the meaning of all "good" life subjected him to fearsome perplexities, frustrations, sorrows, and angers. Mill was far too skilled and far too objective an observer of reality to conceal from himself the fact that "human life is governed" neither by love nor by Harriet nor by "the good principle," but rather by inalienable laws, which require that there be "alteration" and, ultimately, death in every "structure." Mill's power to love gave him much joy. However, his manner of loving often caused him to experience debilitating doubts about life's meanings and pleasures.

I need hardly add that the extremity of his devotion made Mill believe that he was hopelessly dependent upon Harriet. He did not suppose that he could endure life without her. Unfortunately, this was a supposition that became put to test. After many months of poor health, Harriet died on November 3, 1858. Her death gravely threatened the stability and the peace which she had given her husband. In a letter to his friend W. T. Thornton, Mill provides a vivid sense of the fearsome torment and terror which the loss of his wife visited upon him. "It is doubtful" he declares, "if I shall ever be fit for anything public or private again. The spring of my life is broken."[40] In 1859 he wrote: "Melancholy . . . is the groundplan of my life [now] and is always in the depths whatever else may be on the surface."[41] Alexander Bain describes how strained and perilous Mill's state of mind became:

> For some months, he saw nobody, but still corresponded actively on matters that interested him. His despondency was frightful. In reply to my condolence, he said 'I have recovered the shock as much as I ever shall. Henceforth, I shall be only a conduit for ideas.'[42]

In letter after letter, in conversation after conversation, Mill indicated that he had been able to keep "melancholy" and "shock" at bay
solely by the means of his love and his marriage. He felt certain that
life lived as a widower could only seem full of solitude and stark
with suffering.

But Mill did not know how resilient he had become. Soon after
Harriet's death he began to build a new "structure," which allowed
him to reorder and to revitalize the terms under which he lived and
worked. In a letter to Arthur Grote, Mill remarked:

Life [is] a blank now that she has disappeared from it. I seem
to have cared for things or persons, events, opinions on the
future of the world, only because she cared for them: the sole
motive that remains strong enough to give any interest to life
is the desire to do what she would have wished. [43]

Mill felt neither ashamed of nor defensive about this exteriorizing of
his "motive" and "desire." In the *Autobiography* he proudly proclaims
that externalizing his energies and impulses became the formal principle and, ultimately, the conscious programme of his existence. He
writes:

I have sought for such alleviation as my state admitted of, by
the mode of life which most enabled me to feel her still near
me. I bought a cottage as close as possible to the place where
she is buried, and there my [stepdaughter] (my fellow-
sufferer and now my chief comfort) and I, live constantly
during a great portion of the year. My objects in life are
solely those which were hers: my pursuits and occupations
those in which she shared, or sympathized, and which are
indissolubly associated with her. Her memory is to me a religion, and her approbation the standard by which, summing
up as it does all worthiness, I endeavour to regulate my life.
(*Autobiography*, 144–45)

It was fully in keeping with the constitution of Mill's psyche that
he could make such an efficient use of Harriet's death and of his own
grief. By this tactic of dedicating himself to "the desire to do what
she would have wished," he preserved his "interest [in] life," his

"strength," and his "energy" in almost their full state of excited engagement. For the remainder of his life Mill assigned the "motive" of memorialization and posthumous "approbation" to all his labors. He existed and he worked in order to pay ongoing tribute to his beloved wife.[44] This was, as always with Mill, a "reverse" or a "negative" source of affect and of will. However, in response to this inverted imagination of "worthiness" he motivated and equipped himself to conduct an intensely active and a supremely useful existence as a writer and as a citizen.

I believe that Harriet made herself "so precious & delightful" to Mill because she helped him complete the long and complex process by which he converted his imagination from its impossible and forbidden Oedipal structure to the more socialized and the more productive order that he expresses in his literature. Harriet appears to have won her husband's mind and heart because she unconsciously agreed to become a symbolization of his father. In so doing, she permitted Mill to love as he always had longed to love: explicitly rather than subconsciously; exuberantly rather than ambivalently and fearfully. Harriet became so important to Mill, I have suggested, because she provided him with the ground upon which he could conclude the arduous and the long-delayed psychological work of his sonship. She offered herself to her husband as the object or the ego-ideal around whom he at last could satisfy his deep need to accept and to explore another person, himself, and "the great questions of feeling & life."

Mill's manner of loving and his manner of mourning may seem from certain points of view excessive or even hysterical. Some readers may conclude that the Mills' entire relationship was based upon grossly neurotic stimulations. Perhaps this was the case. This does not mean, however, that there was anything ungenuine or unlovely about either the marriage or the energies that the marriage released. Harriet and Mill recognized and accepted one another for what they each were able to be. They loved one another as selflessly and as intimately as they could, and they gave one another considerable happiness. Particularly in Mill's case it seems appropriate to suggest that his undoubtedly overdetermined devotion was a triumph of health and intelligence. Given his history and its devastating consequences, it is surprising and admirable that he could love at all.

That he could love so passionately is an indication of the essential soundness and the great vitality of his character.

In the surround of loving guidance with which Harriet supplied him, Mill produced extraordinary work during the 1840s and the 1850s. I do not command enough space in this essay to explore the meanings, the forms, and the motivations of each of the writings that have made Mill famous. I shall examine, rather, the broad structures and the general purposes of his mature literature. I shall conclude my discussion by examining in some detail *On Liberty* and the *Autobiography,* the two works that Mill himself believed were his most accomplished, his most important, and his most personal creations.

_____4

Resolution and Independence

Mill's literature is anything but monotonic. His work does sound, however, a single recurring theme. As his subject Mill almost always takes the uses and the abuses of power. In almost all his texts he celebrates the claims of moderate liberty and exposes the perils of immoderate authority. His language never is belligerent. But he assumes his ground bluntly and boldly. In the *Principles of Political Economy,* for example, he declares:

> Whatever theory we adopt respecting the foundations of the social union, and under whatever political institutions we live, there is a circle around every individual human being, which no government, be it that of one, or a few, or of the many, ought to be permitted to overstep: there is a part of the life of every person who has come to the years of discretion within which the individuality of that person ought to remain uncontrolled either by any other individual or by the public collectively.[1]

This characteristic passage reveals much about the intentions, the values, and the strategies that shape Mill's mature discourse. Certainly nothing is more conspicuous about the paragraph than its idea of itself as a collocation. The text takes its identity and its authority from its sense that it is speaking as the voice of an entire civilization's experience and will. "We"; "there is"; "every individual human being"; "every person": the author of this language addresses us as a completely collectivized consciousness. Mill represents his opinions and his desires as if they expressed the disinterested judgment of the entire society, rather than the insights, the impressions, and the wishes of a single, sensual individual. The passage's subject matter is as collectivized as its voice. Mill refers to the aggregation of people. He concerns himself neither with particular persons nor with himself, but with the totality of humankind. In his literature as in his life, Mill could not often allow himself to feel comfortably stimulated by individualism. He usually could permit himself to conceive only of the possibilities that are presented by corporateness and culture.

This commitment to community may be seen throughout the paragraph. Mill gives a gravely disturbing account of civilization's power to molest "every individual human being." Yet he feels certain that civilization constitutes the "foundation" of every man's "individuality." No matter how deeply he fears "the social union," it never occurs to him to consider if there may not be some other way of life which is preferable to that which is conferred upon men by "institutions," by "government," and by "the public collectively." What is more, Mill feels convinced that the dangerous but indispensable "social union" is predominantly intellectualistic in both its constitution and its modes of operation. He insists that "whatever theory we adopt" about the social surround decisively affects the structures of civilization, and by this means directly conditions "the life of every person." Here, as so often in his work, Mill contends that the intelligence with which we think determines the wisdom, the dignity, and the pleasure with which we may live. We find ourselves in the presence of an imaginative artist who identifies citizenship and rationalism as the essential metaphysical activities of man. We find ourselves confronting a writer who seems always to have hoped and always to have believed that logic rather than instinct one day might become the governing principle of human thought and human behavior.[2]

The more closely we examine the paragraph I have cited, the more peculiar it seems. The writing is at once socialized and subversive, submissive and seditious. Mill contends that civilization both prohibits and provides a "foundation" for "individuality." He asserts that we must become simultaneously in "union" with other persons and psychologically "uncontrolled" by them. He maintains that the nature and the purpose of "political institutions," "government," and "the public collectively" is to regulate but not ultimately to restrict "the life of every person."

The antinomies that shape this somewhat confused argument closely parallel those that had structured Mill's personal experience. We have seen that Mill both welcomed and feared his father's overwhelming authority; that he needed and consciously cherished James's "government," but that he subconsciously hated and longed to resist James's usurpation of his autonomy. Here, as in his earlier essays, Mill moves to resolve the disabling contradictions that his sonship had imposed upon him by accepting contradictoriness as an inevitable and an appropriate fact of life. He expresses both of his opposing convictions. He proclaims that "government, be it that of one, or a few, or of the many" may stifle *and* liberate "the individuality" of "every person." He asserts that a man may be at the same moment wholly ruled and completely free. He contends that a person may be simultaneously a conscientious son and an independent, integrated adult. In the *Principles of Political Economy* as in almost every other of his mature works, Mill invokes for public and for personal purposes the principal stratagem of his childhood. He attempts to deal with his conflicts and his ambivalences not by choosing between antithetical interests, but by trying equally to validate those interests' opposed and competing claims.

Mill could accomplish this seemingly impossible denial of contradiction because he first detoxified the contradictions' incendiary subliminal content. In the paragraph before us, he engages the volatile subject of "individuality" by distorting it. He represents the idea of absolute social power—for Mill himself, the idea of his father—as the "government . . . of one, or a few, or of the many." This locution produces a number of important transformations. Identifying his father as an abstractive force that is embodied in "government" permits Mill symbolically to recognize the sovereignty and the ascendancy of his parent. At the same time, however, the maneuver allows him to regularize his relationship with that authoritative and frightening figure. He can think of power and of submission in other than purely personal terms. He can exclaim that *"every* person" needs and more or less gladly consents to something like his own experience of "government."

We note, too, that even as he confirms the necessity and the naturalness of his in fact radically abnormal relationship with his parent, Mill tentatively liberates himself from the relationship's most restricting conditions and requirements. As in his earlier essays, he celebrates the claims of familism (or, here, the claims of "the social union"). Yet, in the same sentence in which he pays this dutiful and necessary homage to his progenitor he contends that every person who has come to the years of discretion must be permitted finally to "reign" over his own "life." He accepts the authority of his sire. But he also constructs a separate entitlement for himself. Mill's discreet and ingenious language offers itself as an instrument which allows him perpetually to feel and to behave like a satellite to his father even as he yearns for and works to create an imaginative "circle" of his own.

This seemingly paradoxical, intimately personal impulse may be discerned everywhere in Mill's literature. Even his most forbiddingly public and formalistic work is charged with prosecuting this calm and cautious, necessarily ambivalent and subconscious insurrection against the totalism of his parent's "government." In *A System of Logic,* for example, Mill comments: "We are exactly as capable of making our own character, if we will, as others are capable of making it for us."[3] In *The Principles of Political Economy* he asserts: "Letting alone, in short, should be the general practice: every departure from it, unless required by some great good, is a certain evil."[4] In his more personal writings Mill speaks to similar effect. In his diary he remarks: "Not symmetry, but bold, free expression in all directions is demanded by the needs of modern life and the instincts of modern man."[5] In the *Autobiography* he states that nothing is more important to "man and society [than] a large variety in types of character, [and] giving full freedom to human nature to expand itself in innumerable and conflicting directions" (*Autobiography,* 150). In a letter to John Elliott he declares: "My own motive for writing always has been the desire to define and to excite sympathy for that which I hold to be the highest of all causes, . . . liberty."[6] Throughout his career Mill searched and spoke for a significant but a highly strictured and a highly circumstanced "liberty." His texts strongly advocate "letting alone." With equal force, however, they affirm his father's "circle" of fealty, sublimation, reasonableness, and collectivity. In each of his works the speaking, dreaming, creating voice is Mill's own. Mill's voice operates, though, as a refraction or as an echo of a Word previously spoken by his parent.

This complicated synthesis of independence with dependence achieved its most full and its most inventive form in *On Liberty*. To this bold and brilliant, intensely personal book I now shall turn.

Mill describes the genesis of *On Liberty* in the *Autobiography*. He recalls: "I had first planned on writing it as a short essay in 1854. It was in mounting the steps of the Capital [in Rome], in January, 1855, that the thought first arose of converting it into a volume" (*Autobiography*, 144). On January 15, 1855, he wrote to Harriet:

> The best thing to write & publish at present would be a volume on Liberty. So many things might be brought into it & nothing seems to me more needed—it is a growing need too, for opinion tends to encroach more & more on liberty, & almost all the projects of social reformers in these days are really *liberticide*. . . . If she thinks so I will try to write & publish it in 1856 if my health permits as I hope it will.[7]

A month later he remarked:

> We have got a power of which we must try to make a good use during the few years of life we have left. The more I think of the plan of a volume on Liberty, the more likely it seems to me that it will be read & make a sensation. The title itself with any known name to it would sell an edition. We must cram into it as much as possible of what we wish not to leave unsaid.[8]

This feeling of urgency, this twice-communicated sense of emergency charges the text of *On Liberty* as thoroughly and as dramatically as it shapes Mill's letters about the book. Mill's concern was in part personal: both he and Harriet were suffering from tuberculosis, and their prognoses had become anything but favorable. His alarm, however, was far less for his wife and for himself than for the human community at large. As he wrote *On Liberty* it seemed to Mill that, under the pressure of the profound economic and political changes which had been occurring throughout the world during the nineteenth centry, the experience of freedom and even the desire for freedom was becoming abandoned by most men.

Mill expresses this conviction throughout *On Liberty*. He begins the book by remarking:

> The subject of this essay is . . . Civil or Social Liberty: the nature and limits of the power which can be legitimately exercised by society over the individual. . . . [This subject] is so far from being new, that, in a certain sense, it has divided mankind, almost from the remotest ages; but in the state of progress into which the more civilised portions of the species have now entered, it presents itself under new conditions, and requires a different and more fundamental treatment.[9]

Mill does not for a moment suppose that liberty either can or ought to be absolute. He declares:

> All that makes existence valuable to any one, depends on the enforcement of restraints upon the actions of other people. Some rules of conduct, therefore, must be imposed, by law in the first place, and by opinion on many things which are not fit subjects for the operation of law. What these rules should be is the principal question in human affairs. (6–7)

If this be "the principal question in human affairs," the principal *danger* in human affairs seems to Mill to be the great increase in both formal and informal "restraint" that civilization now routinely imposes upon every person's appropriate autonomy. Throughout *On Liberty* Mill argues that in the modern age society has become progressively more invasive of every individual's humanity. He contends that civilization has developed a perverse and pervasive, almost actively adversary response to distinctive experience. "Reflecting persons [have] perceived," he comments, that "society itself is [now] the tyrant—society collectively over the separate individuals who compose it." He continues:

> It practices a social tyranny more formidable than many
> kinds of political oppression, since, though not usually up-
> held by such extreme penalties, it leaves fewer means of es-
> cape, penetrating much more deeply into the details of life,
> and enslaving the soul itself. Protection, therefore, against the
> tyranny of the magistrate is not enough: there needs protec-
> tion also against the tyranny of the prevailing opinion and
> feeling; against the tendency of society to impose, by other
> means than civic penalties, its own ideas and practices as
> rules of conduct on those who dissent from them; to fetter
> the development, and, if possible, prevent the formation, of
> any individuality not in harmony with its ways." (6)

In the contemporary culture, Mill believes, this social tyrannizing has become more powerful than ever before in history. In a state of barely controlled fear and fury, Mill describes the consequences of this situation:

> I do not mean that [people] choose what is customary in
> preference to what suits their own inclinations. It does not
> occur to them to have any inclination, except for what is
> customary. Thus the mind itself is bowed to the yoke: even in
> what people do for pleasure, conformity is the first thing
> thought of; . . . Peculiarity of taste, eccentricity of conduct,
> are shunned equally with crimes: until by dint of not follow-
> ing their own nature they have no nature to follow: their
> human capacities are withered and starved: they become in-
> capable of any strong wishes or native pleasures. (58)

The peril seems to Mill so extreme that he feels impelled to describe the contemporary experience of life as a situation of momentous his-torical crisis. He indicates that he regards *On Liberty* as both an alarum and a programme for recovery. With all the certitude and zeal of a prophet he exclaims:

[There is now] so great a mass of influences hostile to individuality, that it is not easy to see how it can stand its
ground. . . . If the claims of individuality are ever to be asserted, the time is now, while much is still wanting to complete the enforced assimilation. It is only in the earlier stages
that any stand can be successfully made against the encroach-
ment. . . . If resistance waits till life is reduced *nearly* to one
uniform type, all deviations from the type will come to be
considered impious, even monstrous and contrary to nature.
(69)

Perhaps the most striking conception expressed in these extremely
anxious passages is the idea that liberty and eccentricity have intrin-
sic and identifiable uses. Mill believes that individuality commands
particular sanctions or justifications. Some of these "claims," as he
calls them, are civic or social. It seems to Mill that all significant
advances in human happiness have occurred as the result of certain
individual persons' discoveries of certain specific truths. Mill contends that men and women of genius can develop their powers and
achieve their insights only in those societies in which people feel
themselves encouraged freely to imagine, freely to think, freely to
dispute with one another, and freely to act. He writes:

The initiation of all wise or noble things comes and must
come from individuals; generally at first from some one individual. . . . Europe is, in my judgement, wholly indebted
to [its] plurality of paths for its progressive and many-sided
development. (63, 68)

His perspective, Mill reminds us, is world-historical. His frame of
reference is epochal. In one of the most moving and one of the most
intelligent passages which he ever wrote, Mill observes:

The only unfailing and permanent source of improvement is
liberty, since by it there are as many possible independent
centers of improvement as there are individuals. The progressive principle, however, in either shape, whether as the love
of liberty or of improvement, is antagonistic to the sway of

Custom . . . ; and the contest between the two constitutes
the chief interest of the history of mankind. The greater part
of the world has, properly speaking, no history, because the
despotism of Custom is complete. (66)

Mill is suggesting that he wrote *On Liberty* in order to help rescue
the human race from its tragic refusal to experience history. He is
indicating that he wrote the essay because he wanted to help save
contemporary people from their pathetic and crippling reluctance to
become more curious, more inventive, and more advanced.

This intention assumes an appropriately individualistic reference.
Throughout the essay, Mill advances the idea that the utility of liberty finally is individual rather than social. He repeatedly insists that
life is paramountly personal and private; that we exist principally in
order to develop and to fulfill our own instincts, inclinations, and
abilities. The importance and certainly the wonderfulness of *On Liberty* have chiefly to do with the fact that Mill continually invokes
individuality as his primary value.

Some of his statements to this effect are moderate and conciliatory. Mill sometimes speaks of tolerance as one among many of a
progressive civilization's significant characteristics. He declares, for
example: "Free development of individuality is one of the leading
essentials of well-being; . . . it is not only a co-ordinate element
with all that is designated by the term civilization, instruction, education, culture, but is itself a necessary part and condition of these
things" (54). He observes, similarly: "It is essential that different
persons should be allowed to lead different lives. In proportion as
this latitude has been exercised in any age, has that age been note-
worthy to posterity" (60).

More often, however, Mill speaks more assertively. He insists that
all people have certain sovereign privileges or entitlements; and that
the freedom to think and to behave independently is without question the most important of these rights. He remarks, for instance:

Different persons [require] different conditions for their spiritual development. . . . The same mode of life is a healthy
excitement to one, keeping all his faculties of action and en-
joyment in their best order, while to another it is a distract-
ing burthen, which suspends or crushes all internal life. Such

are the differences among human beings in their sources of
pleasure, their susceptibilities of pain, and the operation on
them of different physical and moral agencies, that unless
there is a corresponding diversity in their modes of life, they
neither obtain their fair share of happiness, nor grow up to
the mental, moral, and aesthetic stature of which their nature
is capable. (64)

Mill believes that this is the central truth of human life. In a mood
of the highest and most solemn conviction, he cries out:

It really is of importance, not only what men do, but also
what manner of men they are that do it. Among the works of
man, which human life is rightly employed in perfecting and
beautifying, the first in importance surely is man himself.
Supposing it were possible to get houses built, corn grown,
battles fought, causes tried, and even churches erected and
prayers said, by machinery—by automatons in human
form—it would be a considerable loss to exchange for these
automatons even the men and women who at present inhabit
the more civilised parts of the world, and who assuredly are
but starved specimens of what nature can and will produce.
Human nature is not a machine to be built after a model,
and set to do exactly the work prescribed for it, but a tree,
which requires to grow and develop itself on all sides, according to the tendency of the inward forces which make it a
living thing. (56)

Mill's sense of persuasion is so strong and his consciousness of crisis is
so great that he becomes almost bellicose in his assertiveness. In a
condition of, for him, very extreme emotion he declares: "There is
no reason that all human existence should be constructed on some
one or some small number of patterns. If a person possesses any tol-
erable amount of common sense and experience, his own mode of
laying out his existence is the best, not because it is the best in itself,
but because it is his own mode" (64).

Never before had Mill spoken so powerfully. Never before had he
given so clear an indication of his own opinions and values. Throughout *On Liberty,* Mill allows himself intimately and vehemently to de-

fine what he thinks men should become, and what he thinks life should be like. He believes, he tells us, in "human freedom and advancement" (105). He believes in "the human faculties of perception, judgment, discriminative feeling, mental activity, [and] moral preference" (55). He believes in "great energies guided by vigorous reason, and strong feelings controlled by a conscientious will" (65–66). He hopes, he tells us, for "more truth and justice" (50). He expects "a more enlightened conduct, and better taste and sense in human life" (61). He wants men to experience "a much livelier feeling of the meaning of their [creeds]" (41). He wants society to become pervaded with "the intelligent and living apprehension of [truth]" (43). He wants human beings to "be forever stimulating each other to increased exercise of their higher faculties, and increased direction of their feelings and aims towards wise instead of foolish, elevating instead of degrading, objects and contemplations" (71). He wants everyone to resist and to repudiate the increasing mechanicalness of contemporary existence. He wants "the general average of mankind" (65) to believe in, to long for, and to achieve "a greater fulness of life" (60).

Mill speaks, in short, for what he calls "character" (57). He hungers for "great," "vigorous," "strong," "enlightened," perfectly individuated, extremely animated life. Mill feels certain that the source and the site of this, our proper "character," is our intelligence. Throughout *On Liberty* he contends that the intelligence is the defining property of a man, "the inward force" that makes a person "a living thing" (58). He repeatedly suggests that we are most ourselves in our power to think; and that it is, therefore, in our opportunities to think and in our ability to think that we must command comprehensive, virtually complete independence. Mill is unyielding about this principle. With calm but militant determination he declares:

> The object of this Essay is to assert one very simple principle, as entitled to govern absolutely the dealings of society with the individual in the way of compulsion and control. . . . The principle is, that the sole end for which mankind are warranted, individually or collectively, in interfering with the liberty of action of any of their number, is self-protection. That the only purpose for which power can be

rightfully exercised over any member of a civilised community, against his will, is to prevent harm to others. . . . The
only part of the conduct of any one, for which he is amenable
to society, is that which concerns others. In the part which
merely concerns himself, his independence is, of right, absolute. Over himself, over his own mind and body, the individual is sovereign. (10–11)

This is exceptionally firm, exceptionally certain discourse. We are
reading an author who has accomplished absoluteness in his opinions
and assurance in his style. Conviction and confidence intersect
throughout the essay. In paragraph after paragraph, Mill conceives
and speaks with extraordinary fluency and assertiveness. His position is unyielding. But his tone is gentle. With force but also with
tenderness he writes:

This, then, is the appropriate region of human liberty. It
comprises, first, the inward domain of consciousness; demanding liberty of conscience in the most comprehensive
sense; liberty of thought and feeling; absolute freedom of
opinion and sentiment on all subjects, practical and speculative. . . . Secondly, the principle requires liberty of tastes
and pursuits; of framing the plan of our life to suit our own
character, of doing as we like, subject to such consequences as
may follow, without impediment from our fellow-creatures,
so long as what we do does not harm them, even though they
should think our conduct foolish, perverse, or wrong. (13)

Mill concludes his manifesto with a contrapuntal flourish. Calmly,
concretely, unequivocally he states: "The only freedom which deserves
the name, is that of pursuing our own good in our own way, so long
as we do not attempt to deprive others of theirs, or impede their
efforts to obtain it. Each is the proper guardian of his own health,
whether bodily, or mental and spiritual" (14).

How much Mill has achieved. The man who once believed that
he must live as a vassal to his father has identified individualism and
liberty as the fundamental necessities of human existence. The man
who once believed that spontaneity is dangerous and perhaps even
pathological has identified free "thought and feeling" as the basal

requirements of life. The man who once welcomed "compulsion" and who once relished "control" has identified "independence" and unhindered "participation" (13) as the most natural, the most enjoyable, and the most indispensable of our rights.

There is nothing sentimental or cavalier about his creed. Mill does not advocate license or anarchy. He experiences no infatuation with ideas or with actions that are "foolish, perverse, or wrong." He believes in appropriate restraint. He believes in obligated relationships with "our fellow-creatures." His enthusiastic inclination to accommodate other people, his cheerful willingness to submit to legitimate government, makes the very essence of his attitude and of his ideology. In *On Liberty,* Mill imagines and expresses an entirely liberal experience. But he speaks for an earned, a sophisticated, and an arduous liberty.

On Liberty marks, I believe, the culmination of Mill's development as a philosopher, as an artist, and as a person. As he conceived and wrote the essay, Mill finally established a just and stimulating compromise between the demands of his socialness and the claims of his character. He granted "a sphere of action" (13) to each. He formed a "plan of . . . life" in which his conduct could remain under appropriate "compulsion and control" while his consciousness became committed to "absolute freedom of opinion and sentiment on all subjects." In creating this wise and salubrious balance between dependence and autonomy, Mill fulfilled his lifelong desire to live as a loyal son and yet to become "the proper guardian of his own health." As he composed *On Liberty,* as he shaped his ingenious synthesis of seemingly opposed interests and needs, Mill emancipated himself from his terrible anxieties and liberated, at last, his prodigious powers of "thought and feeling." [10]

Mill seems to have realized how much he had achieved for himself in *On Liberty.* It is for this reason, I believe, that the essay is such a convinced and such a moving work. In *On Liberty,* Mill behaves as a person who has discovered a transcendent truth. He speaks in the sublimely certain and exultant tones of Matthew, or Lao-tse, or the Bodhisattva. He writes as a man who has found a Way: a way of perceiving, a way of knowing, and a way of being human.

At certain points in *On Liberty,* Mill almost consciously addresses this possibility. Early in the essay, for example, he remarks:

It is, perhaps, hardly necessary to say that [my] doctrine is meant to apply only to human beings in the maturity of their faculties. We are not speaking of children, or of young persons below the age which the law may fix as that of manhood or womanhood. Those who are still in a state to require being taken care of by others, must be protected against their own actions as well as against external injury. (11)

He later comments:

Nobody denies that people should be so taught and trained in youth as to know and benefit by the ascertained results of human experience. But it is the privilege and proper condition of a human being, arrived at the maturity of his faculties, to use and interpret experience in his own way. It is for him to find out what part of recorded experience is properly applicable to his own circumstances and character. (56)

Throughout *On Liberty,* Mill declares that he has outgrown what he calls his "nonage" (11). He proclaims to himself, to the world, and to his dead father that he has "arrived at the maturity of his faculties" and that he will from this time onward "use and interpret experience in his own way." Mill accepts his childhood and his youth with gratitude, dignity, and love. But he also defines his past, with all its dreadful torments and inhibitions, as a purely preliminary, wholly "protective" stage in his life. He freely assumes the many burdens of his earlier years. But he moves forward in *On Liberty* to claim "the privilege and proper condition" of his adulthood.

On Liberty long has been recognized as a book that is unusually liberal and unusually intelligent in its ideas about freedom. We are in a position to realize that *On Liberty* is remarkable for another reason. Mill's celebration of responsible independence is remarkable, we may understand, because it is the achievement of a man who had been radically repressed. It is a singular and a salient work in part because it is the creation of a person who had been required to fear and to despise liberty. It is the creation of a person who had been taught to equate independence with isolation and individualism with insignificance. To write this daring and intensely personal treatise Mill had to overcome—or, as I have put it, he had to out-grow—his entire experience. In effect he had to reinvent his imagination. He had to challenge and to change everything he ever before had believed about order, duty, purpose, and love.

We cannot fail to feel moved by the sheer inventiveness that shapes and fuels *On Liberty*. Nor can we fail to feel moved by the intense hunger for life that made it possible for Mill to conceive of and to demand "liberty of conscience in the most comprehensive sense." We already regard *On Liberty* as a significant event in the history of opinion. I believe that we also should regard this courageous and thrilling book as a significant event in the history of a very great creative artist.

*—I learn every day by fresh instances,
that only when I have a pen in
my hand can I make language and
manner the true image of my thoughts.*

_____**5**

"Language and Manner":
The Nature and the Uses of Authorship

I have not meant to suggest
that Mill made himself a completely healthy or a completely free
man by writing *On Liberty.* As he imagined and composed the book,
he concluded many exceptionally important evolutions in his character and in his consciousness. But he could not liberate himself from
the principal patterns of his psychology. Throughout his life Mill
remained a neurotically dependent person. Particularly, he felt exorbitantly attached and obligated to his wife—as, earlier, he had felt
extravagantly devoted to his father.

Mill never felt demoralized by his continuing dependency. He
was proud of his compulsive reliance upon Harriet; and he believed
that his relationship with her was as healthy and as creative as it was
fulfilling. It seemed to him that each of his works, and especially *On
Liberty,* should be regarded as a testament to the wholesomeness and
the fecundity of his relationship with his wife. In the *Autobiography,*
for example, he declares:

The 'Liberty' was more directly and literally our joint production than anything else which bears my name, for there was not a sentence of it that was not several times gone through by us together, turned over in many ways, and carefully weeded of any faults, either in thought or expression, that we detected in it. It is in consequence of this that, although it never underwent her final revision, it far surpasses, as a mere specimen of composition, any thing which has proceeded from me either before or since. (*Autobiography*, 149–50)

Mill believed so thoroughly in the superiority of his wife's powers to his own that he refused to revise the manuscript of *On Liberty* after Harriet's death. He explains:

After my irreparable loss one of my earliest cares was to print and publish the treatise, so much of which was the work of her whom I had lost, and consecrate it to her memory. I have made no alteration or addition to it, nor shall I ever. Though it wants the last touch of her hand, no substitute for that touch shall ever be attempted by mine. (*Autobiography*, 152)

During the 1850s and 1860s, Mill became far more aware of and far more committed to "the sovereignty of the individual" (*Autobiography*, 150) than ever before in his life. But he continued to be an obsessively submissive person. He continued to envelop his imagination and his intelligence in the comforting, controlling surround of his wife's symbolically parental mentality.

I believe that we should interpret Mill's continuing overreaction to Harriet as an element of his liberation. In *On Liberty*, we recall, Mill had written: "It is essential that different persons should be allowed to lead different lives. . . . In each person's concerns his individual spontaneity is entitled to free exercise" (*On Liberty*, 60, 71). Dependency evidently was Mill's preferred mode of independence. His overdetermined manner of loving apparently became the form of feeling that gave his "individual spontaneity" its most satisfying and its most fertile "exercise." As he composed *On Liberty*, Mill allowed himself to achieve more freedom and more fluency than he ever before had dared to desire. But he could not make himself—he did not want to make himself—absolutely emancipated. Until his death in 1873 Mill carried out the complicated programme of his psychology. He "balanced" or synthesized his impulse to become free with his impulse to become subsumed into another person. He accepted and cherished the experience of being an individual. However, being an individual necessarily involved for Mill the experience of being subconsciously absorbed in another individual.

Throughout the remaining years of his life, Mill's literature became at least as complex in its motivations and its compensations as his continuing relationship with Harriet. Indeed, the act of writing seems to have become for Mill coessential with the act of living. His behaviors as a writer seem to have become virtually the sole means by which Mill confronted himself and interacted with other people. Until the end of his life, the single most important way in which this inventive but damaged man comprehended and presented his personality was by creating his seemingly impersonal but in fact extremely intimate, unconsciously sensual literature.

As we reflect upon Mill's extraordinary commitment to the art of writing, we naturally find ourselves wishing to know something specific about the nature and the meanings of the language which he invented. We want to know what sorts of words, phrases, syntaxes, and sounds seemed to him expressive, truthful, and interesting. We want to know what kind of stylist—what kind of artist—John Mill ultimately became.

As we read his treatises, journals, and letters we discover that as a stylist Mill wanted, more than anything else, to unite abstractness with immediacy. We learn that, throughout his career, he tried to identify himself, the world, and other people as a set of significant but essentially lexical or merely verbal phenomena. It became Mill's primary project as a writer and as a person to suggest that the universe is a dispassionate, logical, and almost purely phrasal domain; but a domain which may be responded to with profound emotionality. Mill's poetics continually manifest the politics and the persuasions of *On Liberty*. His writing repeatedly explores the possibility that an individual may be outwardly repressed and inwardly inventive, externally conformist and internally emancipated.

This is manifestly true of Mill's public discourse. We have seen that in "The Spirit of the Age," "Civilization," "Bentham," "Coleridge," and *On Liberty*, Mill's subjects and stylistics are at the same moment general and personal, abstractive and passionate. This is even more true of his private discourse. In most of the more than twenty-three hundred of his letters that have survived, Mill makes a remarkable attempt to depict the entire scheme of creation as a fundamentally neutral organization: an immense stock of suggestive syllables and involving words. Simultaneously, however, he represents his own emotions, convictions, and experiences as strongly charged, unmistakably individualistic "spheres of action." From his correspondence we may see that Mill's language became coextensive with his temperament. We may see that in his prose, as in his instincts and his intelligence, dissociation and identification became inseparably fused. From both his public and his private literature, we learn that Mill became as an artist precisely what he became as a man: a most intricate combination of absolute sublimation and absolute spontaneity.

We may discern much about Mill's purposes and practices as a stylist by examining some characteristic examples of his work as an epistler. I first shall consider a letter that is merely occasional: one among a host of other, quite similar documents. During the winter and the spring months of 1854–55, Mill made an extensive tour of the Continent. When he arrived in Syracuse in March 1855, he wrote to his wife an exhaustively detailed account of his journey. As we read his letter, we discover that Mill could accept and share his experience only by completely literalizing the place, the day, and his own perceptions and emotions. His writing functions as a transcription or a voiceover which affirms the validity of his experience by registering as recorded language everything that he saw, thought, and felt. The letter seems much like an American sports broadcast, in which the event of sport is not believed to have become fully concluded or wholly meaningful until it has been described, verbally reacted to, and repeatedly replayed. Mill writes:

> I do not think there is any town, not even Athens, which I
> have so much feeling about as Syracuse: it is the only ancient
> town of which I have studied, & known & understand, the
> localities: so nothing was new or dark to me. I cannot look at
> that greater harbour which my window in the Albergo del
> Sole looks directly upon, without thinking of the many de-
> spairing looks which were cast upon the shores all round (as
> familiar to me as if I had known them all my life) by the

armament of Nicias & Demosthenes. That event decided the fate of the world, most calamitously—If the Athenians had succeeded they would have added to their maritime supremacy all the Greek cities of Sicily & Italy, Greece must soon have become subordinate to them & the empire thus formed in the only way which could have united all Greece, might have been too strong for the Romans & Carthaginians. Even if they had failed & got away safe, Athens would never have been subdued by the Peloponnesians, but would have remained powerful enough to prevent Macedonia from emerging from obscurity, or at all events to be a sufficient check on Philip & Alexander. Perhaps the world would have been now a thousand years further advanced if freedom had thus been kept standing in the only place where it ever was or could then be powerful. I thought & felt this till I could have cried with regret & sympathy. [1]

This is a startling document. Mill is suggesting that Syracuse has intelligibility and appeal for him primarily because in its contemporary form it is compatible with the histories of the city which he previously has "studied." He does not want to "know & understand" Syracuse by looking "directly upon" its actual "harbour." He prefers to reconstruct the town's "localities" as recalled literature. He scarcely feels engaged by the city's sights, scents, and sounds. He feels drawn, rather, to a narrative record of "despairing looks" and heroic "armament." He feels intrigued less by the city's living reality than by its recorded historiography. For Mill, it seems, the city's and his own character most significantly defined themselves in the fixed and finite idiom of written language. For Mill, it appears, "localities," occurrences, and his own emotions had to be chronicled before he could feel them to have been authentic and important.

Mill eventually invested this impulse with the full force of an instinction. He ultimately found it *necessary* to verbalize his experiences. He seems to have felt conscious of this circumstance. In 1852 he wrote: "I learn every day by fresh instances, that only when I have a pen in my hand can I make language and manner the true image of my thoughts." [2] In 1840 he declared: "We scribblers are apt to put not only our best thoughts but our best feelings into our writings, or at least if the things are *in* us they will not come out of us so well or so clearly through any other medium." [3] In 1855 he remarked to his wife: "It is writing to [you] in the evening about the day's incidents that makes them interesting." [4]

If Mill was to some extent aware of his need to literalize his existence, he was almost completely unaware of the extent and the systematism of this compulsion. He seems to have been unconscious of the fact that he felt impelled to reorganize virtually all of his life's occasions and events into formal "language and manner." He seems to have been unaware of the fact that he habitually verbalized not only his most rarefied but also his most quotidian ideas and impulses.

As we read Mill's correspondence, we discover that not even his entertainments and avocations escaped this process of compulsive literalization. Mill was, for example, an avid hiker and botanist. But he evidently could neither encounter nor enjoy the countrysides he explored until he composed letters about them. He felt it necessary to write accounts that recreated the landscapes and the activities he loved as sets of sublingual scripts or subverbal narratives. Let us consider the following instance. After an apparently delightful hike, Mill writes:

> We have got here from Canterbury today, having spent eight hours on foot, walking and botanizing, besides seeing Canterbury Cathedral & Richborough by the way. Though these two days journeys were by far the least promising botanically speaking, of our whole route, we have found a great many plants, and though there is not yet much that is quite new to me, I have filled up an immense number of gaps in my Kent Flora. [5]

Mill wants to achieve much more here than merely to describe an expedition into Kent. He wants as well to represent and to apprehend Kent as a sort of text: a text comprised of a precise number of identifiable "flora" and recognizable edifices. He seems to want to confront the region and his experience of it by collecting or, as it were, by reading what might be called the complete edition of its literary works.

As with Kent, so with the capital cities of Europe—and even his own home. After making a voyage to Rome, Mill writes: "There are now hardly any pictures of note in Rome which I have not seen, &

many of the finest repeatedly. As it is now probable that I shall not return to Rome, I am glad to have made the impression complete and strong."[6] From his home in Blackheath he one day comments: "The birds who had begun singing have left off, though there are now great numbers of them. The other day looking out of my bedroom window I perceived five bullfinches perched on a thorn near the dining room window."[7] Mill attempted to experience almost all places, events, and emotions in essentially the same way. Throughout his career he tried to fulfill the functions of his "individuality" by transforming all his impressions, judgments, and feelings into precise, complete, and thoroughly comprehended verbal accounts.

In all his work as a writer, Mill tried to identify both the great world and his own personality as a literature written in historical "armament," venerable buildings, collectable "flora," "pictures of note," and specific numbers of bullfinches caught chirping in particular clumps of thorn. He created books, essays, letters, and journals primarily for the reason that contemporary persons might now photograph, videotape, or tape record: in order to impart chosen and controllable associations onto passing transactions and phenomena. Throughout his life Mill accomplished cognition, coherence, and pleasure by converting the complex materials of his consciousness into the manageable structures and the manipulable energies of written speech. A profoundly creative artist, he engaged the universe and manufactured a character by authoring the reality that he wanted, and needed, to encounter.

The reality that Mill needed to encounter was a reality in which he could believe himself to be included in the processes of more normally ordered life. Obese people often unconsciously believe that they can join themselves to the universe by consuming all of the universe's edible substances. An obese person often hopes to compensate for feeling excluded from life by attempting symbolically to take the world into himself. Mill was not physically obese. However, he experienced certain elements of the psychology of obesity. In the making of his literature, Mill behaved as though he hoped to project himself into the world by reading and recording—by consuming and reconstituting—all of the world's ways of verbalizing itself. The fat man tries to experience life by ingesting and recomposing its foodstuffs. Mill tried to experience life by ingesting and recomposing its languages.

The diction that Mill created was crucial to the success of this project. I refer particularly to the elaborate specificity of his prose. I can think of no other major English stylist whose work is so routinely and so rigorously delineative. Mill constantly requires his writing to abstract and to particularize. He obsessively tries to define distinguishing characteristics and typifying principles. Mill appears most accomplished and most satisfied as an artist when he can declare what a person, a place, or a thing exactly and forever is. His discourse frequently assumes an almost explicitly taxidermal intention and tone: he often seems to want to seize, to stuff, and to mount his subjects. Let us consider again the passage I cited earlier: "The other day looking out of my bedroom window I perceived five bullfinches perched on a thorn near the dining room window." There is a strange compulsiveness in this gratuitous locating and naming. The bedroom window; the dining room window; bullfinches, not wrens or sparrows; exactly five birds, not four or six; the precise, almost prissy verb "perceived." Surely anyone else would have written (if anyone else would have written anything at all about such an occasion): "I saw a few birds outside." Mill's superfluously specific language effectively terminates activeness. The bullfinches become fixed and frozen by the phrases which so minutely define them. The prose that situates the creatures also surrounds them, demystifies and discreates them. The alluring, living birds are transformed into sheerly semantic entities.

The author becomes as neutered by this discourse as his subject. The speaker who finds and arrests the birds deliberately devitalizes himself. He makes himself sound like a Casaubon or a Gradgrind. Mill was an heroically tolerant and a wonderfully exploratory person. But in his writing he usually required himself to seem almost affectless. The purposes that charge and the effects that environ his work often appear to be intentionally aligned against changeableness, chance, and mystery. The diction makes the writer sound frightened of spontaneity and fearful of genuine complexity. In this respect the universe that Mill represents in his literature can seem invasive of life, somewhat dull, and even, at times, parochial. Certain readers may go so far as to conclude that Mill was a sexless man who created a sexless art.

It rather was the case, I believe, that the concreteness and the quietism of his prose style became the means by which Mill controlled and expressed his kind of sexuality. We have observed that by literalizing almost everything about his life, Mill created a universe in which all forces, events, and things seemed coherent and regulable. The intelligibility and the manageableness that this unconscious tactic imposed upon the external world seem to have extended to Mill's internal world. As he wrote his seemingly neutral, obsessively categorizing literature, Mill apparently produced a highly consoling delusion: the delusion that by writing his calm and certain prose he could desensitize all the potentially explosive materials which were embedded in his subconscious psychology. On no other terms did Mill believe that he could risk participating in life. He seems to have based his entire capacity to function and to feel upon his faith in his ability to divert his volatile libidinal drives onto the reassuringly safe apparatus of his exaggeratively formal art. In this sense, writing and loving were closely allied activities for Mill. He seems to have conceived of his purposes as an author and his passions as a person in conspicuously similar ways.

For ourselves the scientism of Mill's prose may operate in such a way as to limit the energy and the effectiveness of his work. Some readers may find that Mill's writing is excessively cerebral, or insufficiently spontaneous. For Mill himself, however, the inhibitions of his art became the essence and the guarantor of his identification. He did not believe that he could develop the "circle" of his individuality in any more direct or any more natural a manner. What may seem to some readers as a dispassionate or a soulless literature seemed to the author himself to be a singularly intimate, sensual, and even primal discourse.

There is another respect in which the act of authorship seemed to Mill a normalizing or a regularizing activity. In the *Autobiography* he reports that in his work as a writer he always felt a great "readiness and eagerness to learn from everybody, and to make room in my opinions for every new acquisition by adjusting the old and the new to one another" (*Autobiography*, 150). Mill seems to have imagined that this "willingness to learn from everybody" brought him into at least metaphorical communion with everybody. He seems to have supposed that writing his syncretic or "joining" texts involved him directly and powerfully with other people and with "all the practical departments of life" (*Autobiography*, 127). For Mill, it appears, writing literature made for a broad and general experience of society.

Mill did not want his experience of society to become more genuine or more demanding. He never became confident and comfortable in his relationships with other people. He could alter many of his circumstances and many of his perceptions; but he could not change his history or the temperament which his history had produced. He could not convert himself into a truly convivial person. Throughout his life, Mill's responses to other people were usually hesitant and impersonal. His manner was almost always guarded and polite. He greatly preferred discoursing to encountering and engaging. He always regarded disputation and writing as his primary interactional behaviors. Mill rescued himself from solitude and despair. But he never became like Boswell or Dickens. He never became a man who craved and who delighted in the company of other persons.

Mill knew that his sociableness was reluctant and intellectualistic. He knew that he regarded citizenship and fraternity rather more as accepted obligations than as passionate preferences. He made no effort to conceal or to deny this fact. In 1860, for example, he wrote to one of his few close friends:

> The truth is that though I detest society for society's sake, yet
> when I can do anything for the public objects I care about by
> seeing & talking with people I do not dislike it. At the moment of going to do it, I feel it a bore, just as I do taking a
> walk or anything else that I must & ought to do when not
> wishing to do it. But I believe the little additional activity &
> change of excitement does me good, & that it is better for
> me to try to serve my opinions in other ways as well as with
> a pen in my hand.[8]

Mill had built his psychology upon sublimation and displacement. Throughout the remaining years of his life he continued to believe that rigidity and deflection were necessary for his survival. He always found it easier and safer to control the "activity" and the "excitement" of social intercourse by approaching others from behind the shield of his writings. Mill realized that the experience of society which his literature made available to him was inverse, and perhaps even perverse. But communion with other people on even these limited and somewhat distorted terms apparently proposed itself to him as a great relief from his earlier condition of isolation and terror. If "society for society's sake" always affected him as a burden and "a bore," the feeling of having at least some fellowship with other people, the sense of having at least certain "public objects," always seemed to Mill a salvation from the pathos and the pain of his previous aloneness.

We may identify at least one other extremely important use to which Mill put his "opinions" and his literature. In his *Autobiography,* Mill indicates that from his endeavors as an author he derived more than an impression of safety, normalcy, and community with other people. He also achieved, he suggests, a sense of personal "authority," "power," and "ascendancy." In an extremely aroused passage, he declares:

> The mass of mankind, including even their rulers in all the
> practical departments of life, must, from the necessity of the
> case, accept most of their opinions on political and social
> matters, as they do on physical, from the authority of those
> who have bestowed more study on those subjects than they
> generally have it in their power to do. . . . The moral and
> intellectual ascendancy, once exercised by priests, must in
> time pass into the hands of philosophers. (*Autobiography,* 127)

This is entirely new ground for Mill. He is contending that the work of moral philosphers—his own work—is indispensable to human development. He is laying claim to the right not simply to participate in human life, but also to interpret, to organize, and even to direct other people's "political and social" affairs. Throughout his childhood and youth Mill had conceived of himself as an utterly subservient person. Here, as he comes to a full recognition of his unique abilities, he is identifying himself as a sovereign and a commanding man. He is declaring that he has supplanted his father, and that he has inherited all of his father's imposing prerogatives.

In the final years of his life, the mood and the language in which Mill presented the idea of his "authority" became increasingly more assertive. Often it became actively bellicose. In the *Autobiography,* for example, he finds it possible to refer to the history of philosophy as a long series of "attacks," or an ongoing "hand-to-hand fight." He speaks of his own discourse as a kind of "combat" (*Autobiography,* 163, 176). Earlier I suggested that writing literature fulfilled Mill because it allowed him to continue and to complete his boyhood. We now may observe that his work eventually permitted him to conceive of himself not simply as an autonomous adult but also as a potent adult. His increasingly militaristic descriptions of his art and of himself indicate that Mill gradually came to think of himself less as a son and a servant than as a militant warrior-savant: Achilleus rather than Oedipus.[9]

The conditions under which Mill could tolerate the idea of his own "moral and intellectual ascendancy" were as impersonal and as inverted as those which governed the idea of his sociableness. In a letter to Carlyle he suggests that he could think of himself as having achieved not absolute might or majesty but rather an "equality like every other equality, resolvable into reciprocal superiority."[10] In another letter to Carlyle, Mill comments:

> I think the *vates* himself has often been misunderstood and
> sucessfully cried down for want of a Logician in Ordinary, to
> supply a logical commentary on his intuitive truths . . .
> Now this humbler part is, I think, that which is most suit-
> able to my faculties, as a man of speculation. I am not in the
> least a poet, in any sense; but I can do homage to poetry. I
> can to a very considerable extent feel it and understand it,
> and make others who are my inferiors understand it in pro-
> portion to the measure of their capacity. I believe that such a
> person is more wanted than even the poet himself; that there
> are more persons living who approximate to the latter charac-
> ter than to the former. I do not think myself at all fit for the
> one; I do for the other; your walls I conceive to be
> higher. . . . Poetry is higher than Logic, and [the] union of
> the two is Philosophy.[11]

He later observes:

> If I have any *vocation* I think it is exactly this, to translate the
> mysticism of others into the language of Argument. Have
> not all things two aspects, an Artistic and a Scientific; to the
> former of which the language of mysticism is the most appro-

priate, to the latter that of Logic? The mechanical people, whether theorists or men of the world, find the former unintelligible, & despise it. Through the latter one has a chance of forcing them to respect even what they cannot understand—and that once done, they may be made to *believe* what to many of them must always be in the utmost extent of the term 'things unseen.' This is the service I should not despair of assisting to render, & I think it is even more needed now than works of art, because it is their most useful precursor, & one might almost say, in these days their necessary condition.[12]

In each of these excited passages, Mill is indicating that his writing allowed him symbolically to "approximate" everything he was "not at all fit for" in his personal "faculties" and "capacity." He wrote literature, he declares, to compensate for being perhaps overly "scientific" and "mechanical." He wrote literature, he reports, to "do homage" and "service" to all those "intuitive truths" and passions that he could not more actively feel.

As we read the excerpts before us, we realize that Mill is suggesting even more than this. In a quiet but striking manner he is contending that his disablements in fact have permitted him to accomplish work which has been far more "needed" and far more "useful" than anything which could have been achieved by an author who might appear to be more vigorous or more "Artistic" than himself. Mill is asserting that his excessively inhibited character and his excessively "logical commentary" have given him access to perceptions and to methodologies which are much "higher" and, at least during his current period in history, much more "needed" than any of the "truths" which could have been discerned by "poetry" and its practitioners.

This sense of himself as the true prophet of "intuitive truths" and "'things unseen'" charmed, challenged, and greatly gratified Mill. In one of his happiest letters, he exclaims:

The only thing that I believe I am really fit for, is the investigation of abstract truth, & the more abstract the better. If there is any science which I am capable of promoting, I think it is the science of science itself, the science of investiga-

tion—of method. . . . He who can throw light upon the
subject of method, will do the most to forward that alliance
among the most advanced intellects & characters of the age,
which is the only definite object I ever have in literature or
philosophy so far as I have any *general* object at all. [13]

In an equally exultant letter to his friend John Nichol, Mill declares:

What an immense superiority the *scientific* study of any detached point, by which I mean the habit of viewing it in its
relations to all the rest of the field of which it forms a part,
gives one over the mere dealers in [intuitions] . . . It is a
primitive fallacy to imagine that assurance of truth can be
had by looking at the subject-matter in the *concrete*, without
that process of analysis which men term abstraction. [14]

His own "logical" character, "vocation," and "language" eventually
came to seem to Mill "most appropriate" and more wanted than
anything else seemingly nobler or "higher" in life. Earlier we had
discovered that Mill entered his adulthood as a terrified child, who
believed that he had constantly to deprecate and to subordinate
himself. We now may observe that in the course of his distinguished
career as a "Logician in Ordinary," he gradually achieved a much
healthier and a much happier view of himself. As he created his "*scientific*" art, Mill progressively developed, it appears, an entirely new
perspective upon his powers and upon his worth: a perspective that
allowed him to accept, to admire, and to assert himself as a necessary and heroic man.

I have tried to suggest that in the making of his art as in the
living of his life, the principal impulses to which Mill responded
were the need to believe in himself and the need to achieve a sense of
comfortable and productive involvement with other people. I have
tried to show that Mill became increasingly aware of these subconscious desires or missions, and that he became increasingly confident
about his ability to fulfill them.

Particularly Mill seems to have felt progressively more aware of
his need to comprehend his personal history and its meanings. As he
became more skilled, self-assured, and successful as a critic of philosophy, science, and society, he felt more anxious to understand his

own experience and emotions. He felt determined to achieve a fully resolved response to his wife, to his mother, to his father, and, especially, to himself. In a mood of transcendent inspiration, Mill began in 1853 to write an autobiography. By 1856 he had completed a draft version of what I believe is his most important and his most successful book. He updated the text in 1870; and he reviewed and revised the work until his death in 1873.[15]

To the *Autobiography,* and to the powerful motivations and sentiments that stimulated its composition, I now shall turn.

_____6

'Who Made Me?':
The Autobiography

I have tried to demonstrate that, among his many other talents, Mill had a genius for understanding and for healing the emotions which pained him. I have suggested that writing always functioned for him as a crucial therapeutic activity. Throughout his life, I have argued, Mill comprehended and controlled his anxieties by making them the hidden concern of his literature.

In the *Autobiography,* Mill for the first and for the only time in his life directly confronted himself as a subject. Oddly, this has not always been realized. We admire the *Autobiography* as a description of a family and as an account of an era. We feel moved by the story of Mill's experiences. We do not often acknowledge, however, how troubled and how turbulent a book the *Autobiography* is. Nor do we often react to the fact that the particular things which Mill is finding the power to say about his father, his wife, his work, and himself represent his culminating achievements. The act of writing the *Autobiography* is the *Autobiography's* climactic event. When we read the work, we must understand that writing about himself so frankly and so bravely, engaging himself formally and publicly, is the greatest thing John Mill does in the life that the *Autobiography* records.

As literature the *Autobiography* is, as always with Mill, intricate and difficult. The plotting and the prose initially may seem abstruse or colorless. If we are to receive the book in its full meaning and its full power, we must read the *Autobiography,* as we must read each of Mill's works, carefully and patiently, with sympathy and with an active sense of participation. If we read as Mill needs and asks us to read, we shall find a remarkably intelligent and a remarkably touching book, an experience of literature like no other.

My subject in the discussion that follows will be Mill's place in the story of his own life. As we shall see, his importance and his role in his own history were not necessarily central.[1]

Dickens' *David Copperfield* opens with one of the most shocking lines in literature. David begins the novel and introduces himself by declaring: "Whether I shall turn out to be the hero of my life, or whether that office will be held by anybody else, these pages must show."[2] We cannot help but feel stunned by the extent of David's dissociation and discontent. It unnerves and grieves us that he feels so uncertain about the materials and the meanings of his experience. His situation seems either novelistic or psychotic. This effectively absolute confusion about the significance of circumstances and the authority of selfhood could only occur, we imagine, in a fiction or in a madness.

A strikingly similar moment occurs in the *Autobiography.* In the book's final chapter, Mill comments: "Whoever, either now or hereafter, may think of me and the work I have done, must never forget that it is the product, not of one intellect and consciousness but of three, the least considerable of whom, and above all the least original, is the one whose name is attached to it" (*Autobiography,* 157).[3] The sentence is so disconcerting that we scarcely know how to read it. This calm acceptance of tripartition, this quiet acknowledgment of inconsiderableness and unoriginality, perplexes and frightens us. Mill's conviction that his personality and his experience have evolved as "the product" solely of "intellect and conscience" seems unthinkable. His belief that his sensibility and his "work" have occurred indirectly in response to other persons' "intellect and conscience" seems absurd and abhorrent.

We feel as disturbed by Mill's uses of language as by his perceptions and his judgments. We notice, for example, that he refuses to
employ the personal pronoun. "Me" and "I" reduce themselves to
"it" and "the one whose name is attached to [the text]." We observe
that the sentence's energy and motion emanate from the writer's dep-
recations of himself. We see that the prose derives its order and its
strength from the author's ascriptions of powerlessness and prosaic-
ness to himself. The writing is fascinating. But it is fascinating primarily because of its ability to bewilder and to horrify.

The sentence and its attitudes are characteristic of Mill's work in
the *Autobiography*. Throughout the book he testifies to his lack of
substance. He repeatedly indicates that he is inadequate, unimagi-
native, and somehow impersonal or nonauthoritative in his own life
and work. This is particularly true of the *Autobiography*'s opening
paragraph. Mill begins what he calls his "biographical sketch" of
himself by declaring that his history and his ways of describing it
cannot in themselves seem compelling or even involving. "I do not
for a moment imagine," he remarks, "that any part of what I have to
relate, can be interesting to the public as a narrative, or as connected
with myself." He finds it necessary to legitimize his existence and
his art. He believes, he tells us, that he must make "some mention
of the reasons which have made me think it desirable that I should
leave behind me such a memorial of so uneventful a life as mine" (3).

The "reasons" Mill adduces are odd and alarming. He declares:

> In an age in which education, and its improvement, are the
> subject of more, if not of profounder study than at any for-
> mer period in English history, it may be useful that there
> should be some record of an education which was unusual
> and remarkable. . . . It has also seemed to me that in an age
> of transition in opinions, there may be somewhat both of
> interest and of benefit in noting the successive phases of any
> mind which was always pressing forward, equally ready to
> learn and to unlearn either from its own thoughts or from
> those of others. But a motive which weighs more with me
> than either of these, is a desire to make some acknowledg-
> ment of the debts which my intellectual and moral develop-
> ment owes to other persons. (3)

This is another passage to which we do not immediately understand how to respond. The paragraph almost has no subject. Or, rather, it has a multitude of subjects, which seem both to cooperate and to conflict with one another. The passage appears to concern a man whom we know to have been called John Mill. But the language cannot make its way to Mill's history, or to his character, or even to his name. The writings can identify the man only by drawing together a host of large, indefinite generalizations: "the age"; "an education"; "successive phases"; "any mind"; "debts"; "intellectual and moral development." These abstractions coalesce with one another and advance themselves as the man's substance. John Mill is comprised, we are told, of his "mind" and its "debts" and its "development," all of which came into being during a particular and, we gather, a distinctly unusual period of time in the history of England. The person whom the paragraph tries to make tangible is a man whose materiality derives from the tangibleness of things other than himself. The paragraph simultaneously suggests, however, that this visible, sculpted Mill has become obscured and overwhelmed by the forces which originated him. The man has become dwarfed and ultimately displaced by his "debts" and by his "development." He has become secondary to his origins—so much so that his origins seem far more "eventful," "useful," and "desirable" than the sensibility they collectively have produced. The *Autobiography*'s opening paragraph defines a man who has been both created and destroyed by a set of circumstances which appear to have been too strong and too active for the "mind" they engendered and then abandoned. The brilliant but bizarre paragraph describes a person whose history has made him at once knowable and undiscoverable, conspicuous and undiscernible.

This is Mill's crucial problem in the *Autobiography*. He wants to "think of [himself] and the work [he has] done." But even now, even as he finds himself at the height of his great powers, he does not know how to locate or how to speak about himself. Mill solves this problem, I believe, by circumventing it. Because he does not know how to define his character and his consciousness, he describes his "intellectual and moral development" and the "other persons" who determined it. Because he cannot define the attitudes and the emotions that might have made him tangible, he tries to discuss the evolution or the etiology of his intangibleness. The problem and its resolution are almost insuperably complex. In order to characterize himself, Mill believes that he must acknowledge and represent himself as his lack of character. In order to write about his own substance, he believes that he must write about the successive phases of his reactions to other, more obviously substantial people.

As we have seen, the person who most significantly affected Mill's "development" was Mill's father. It is for this reason, I believe, that the narrative portion of the *Autobiography* opens in the peculiar way it does. Mill declares: "I was born in London, on the 20th day of May 1806, and was the eldest son of James Mill, the author of the *History of British India*" (4). He goes on to write a "biographical sketch" not of himself but of James Mill. He discusses not his own but his parent's history and accomplishments. It seems that even in the final years of his life Mill could approach himself only by engaging and by celebrating the fact of his progenitor.

This tactic is intelligible. A man who believes himself to have been psychically determined by his father will wish to think and to write about his father before he thinks and writes about himself. No matter how intelligible it may be as a psychical act, the stratagem is extremely confusing as the beginning of an autobiography. As we read the material we cannot help but feel perplexed and estranged. Is this, we wonder, a biography or an autobiography? Who is the subject? Who is the writer? Whose life will give the book its issues, events, and energies? Whose personality will give the book its ideas, ideologies, and consciousness?

Our questions are soon answered. We quickly discover that, no matter how puzzling it may be to ourselves, the *Autobiography*'s opening is entirely appropriate to its subject matter. For we learn that the *Autobiography* is primarily concerned with the fact that, even at this late date in his life, Mill does not quite know how to distinguish himself from his parent. We learn that the work is chiefly about the sad and startling fact that, even now, Mill can imagine and discuss his own existence only by imagining, discussing, and trying to participate in his father's existence. The *Autobiography*'s beginning disorients and vexes us. But it ingeniously reports Mill's own lifelong disorientation and anger. It sincerely confesses that confusion and rage are the theme and, as it were, the author of the *Autobiography*. The paragraph tells us that as we read the *Autobiogra-*

phy we shall encounter a hugely bewildered man who is trying to trace "the successive phases" of his terrible persuasion that he is an unidentifiable and an unworthy person—that he is, in particular, a much less actual and a much less excellent person than his imposing father.

There is more which may be said about this paragraph. As we read the *Autobiography,* we discover that the book's strange and seemingly evasive opening identifies two of the sources of Mill's chronic confusion and suffering. "I . . . was the eldest son of James Mill, the author of the *History of British India.*" The sentence's odd language suggests, anything but accidentally, that Mill was engendered, given birth to, and raised by a single parent. The phrasing defines Mill as the son of a father, not the son of a father and a mother. The language seems dispassionate and even, perhaps, resistant. But there is nothing calm or equivocal about Mill's feelings here. As we shall see, he is directly engaging his subliminal interpretation of his situation. His apparent inarticulateness is subconsciously deliberate: he intends to sound bewildered, resentful, and sorrowful. Who was my mother?, the sentence unconsciously is asking. I know who my father was. I know what he did. But who was my mother? Where was she? What did she do? What was she the author of? The contorted, carefully censored writing rigidly controls but does not in the least conceal the writer's bafflement, anguish, and indignation.

The writing also indicates that at least as confusing and painful for Mill as the impression of his father's autogamy was the impression that for his father paternity and authorship seem to have been almost completely correlative activities. The sentence's appositional syntax raises the startling possibility that for James Mill parenting a son and writing a history may have had approximately the same quality and meaning as experiences and as responsibilities. Throughout the *Autobiography*'s first five chapters Mill repeats and extends this dreadful apperception. He goes to considerable lengths to demonstrate that his father regarded him as a species of book. He makes it disturbingly clear that he believed himself to have been not so much parented, loved, and educated as conceived of, written, and edited.

I believe it is for this more than for any other reason that the *Autobiography* has achieved fame. There is a certain titillation in Mill's account of his boyhood situation. It is arousing to read about the absoluteness of Mill's involvement with his father's opinions, values, and modes of consciousness. We feel intrigued as we learn about the extraordinarily primal nature of their relationship. We feel intrigued as we discover how distant and cold James Mill could be within this heated domain. It is not difficult to understand why Mill's descriptions of his family life interest us so much. To one or another extent, we all feel dominated by our parents. Particularly, in one or another way, we feel dominated by our fathers. Mill's experience engrosses us because it seems an almost unthinkable intensification of our own. As we read the *Autobiography* we cannot help but compare our childhood with his. We simultaneously identify and differentiate. We find ourselves wondering, What can it have felt like to have been this subservient to so powerful a parent? What can it have felt like to have been so thoroughly, so utterly fathered?

The *Autobiography* initially does not seem to answer these questions. As we first read the book we may believe that the completeness of Mill's eventual adjustment was as astonishing as the completeness of his early subjection. We feel struck by how neutrally he seems to have reacted to experiences which we think should have outraged him. We wonder at the fact that he continually refers to his boyhood in only the most circumspect terms. We wonder at the fact that he invariably speaks of his father with respect and, often, with worshipful affection. Did he never allow himself to feel victimized? we ask. Did he never feel indignant? Did he feel not a trace of confusion or fear or fury? Can it be that in the case of John Mill sustained psychological abuse precipitated, at least on the conscious level, nothing but acceptance, gratitude, and love?

This possibility puzzles us. But also, I believe, it attracts us. Much of the *Autobiography*'s power to interest and to please derives from its ability to evoke the sense of infinite resilience—or, to put the matter in another way, its ability to evoke the sense of infinitely protracted infantile love. Most of us must mask and moderate the Oedipal hysteria. The *Autobiography* suggests that Mill's experience of the Oedipus complex was unqualified and ecstatic. As he describes it, his entire intrapsychical experience seems to have occurred as an eerie and rather lurid, somehow epical instance of acquiescence. As we first encounter the *Autobiography,* we find ourselves concluding that John Mill may have been a man who was able to yield without resistance and without remorse to the primitive totem of the imperial Father.

It is exactly this which initially seems most compelling about the *Autobiography*. The book delights us, as it seems to have delighted its author, because it summons into formal and excited order all the awe and all the adoration that an infant subliminally directs onto an overly idealized parent. The *Autobiography* strikes us as an urgent and an elemental document because it organizes and releases—and it causes to sound reasonable and healthy—a proscribed instinct that we all experience and that we all long to express. The book is one of the world's most affecting and most important works in part because it examines, directly and deliberately, the forbidden but universally felt pleasures of father-worship. I am suggesting that we initially respond to the *Autobiography* in much the same manner that Mill himself appears to have done. I believe that the text seems to us, as it evidently seemed to Mill, the tableau or the theatre of a fundamental and thrilling taboo.

We soon discover, however, that the *Autobiography* is a much more complex work than we first understand it to be. As we study the text we discover that Mill did respond to the more terrible aspects of his history. We learn that he felt a great deal of anger; but that he expressed his anger covertly and furtively, as if he felt impelled to deny or to deconstruct this reaction. Communicating adjustment and love evidently was agreeable and easy for Mill. When he writes encomia to his parent his prose is quick, certain, and exultant, as if celebrating his father seemed to him appropriate and even holy. His less contented discourse, though, exhibits symptoms of extreme disturbance. Passages in which he expresses objection and suffering sound constrained and reluctant, as if he found, even in his maturity, that angry emotions were confusing or threatening, odious or even intolerable. As we read and reread the *Autobiography,* we discover that Mill controlled the still incendiary material of his hostile responses to his father by glorifying his love and by censoring his rage. He tried, it seems, to conceal certain reactions from himself as well as from his readers. Presumably this was because, even in his adulthood, he did not want to become forced consciously to confront the full contradictoriness of his feelings about his parent and his feelings about his childhood. As we read his deceptive and wily book, we learn that one of the important "motives" that shaped the *Autobiography* was Mill's need to create a mechanism by which he could explore and relieve his continuing ambivalences about his father without ever having coherently to acknowledge that he felt ambivalence.

I may put this complicated matter in another way. The act of writing the *Autobiography* seems to have given Mill a means by which to convert his experience into an existence that he would have preferred to have lived if he could have authored his history. Throughout the *Autobiography* he writes about his boyhood and his youth in such a way as to transform much of the indifference and the restrictiveness that he actually received from James into the love and the liberalness that he wished he had received. He never consciously dissembles. Often, though, he reorders or, as it were, he rewrites his past. He unconsciously denies and reconditions the realities that most deeply wounded him. He describes his parent's interferences, prohibitions, and preoccupations in such a way as to metamorphose James's disregard and abusiveness into symbolic concern and care. In his old age, Mill redefined his childhood feelings of rejection and loneliness into a consciousness of acceptance and inclusion. He treated his fearsome sense of isolation as a happy awareness of communication and communion. Mill recalled—or, I am suggesting, he subconsciously invented—a life that he craved but that he did not have. For this reason the *Autobiography* should be read, I believe, as a work less of reminiscence than of reconstruction and rehabilitation.

We may observe this process of honest and earnest self-deception throughout the *Autobiography*. Early in the narrative, for example, Mill comments: "[My father] was often, and much beyond reason, provoked by my failure in cases where success could not have been expected; but in the main his method was right, and it succeeded" (19). He continues:

> My recollection . . . is almost wholly of failures, hardly ever of success. It is true, the failures were often in things where success in so early a stage of my progress, was almost impossible. . . . In this [my father] seems, and perhaps was, very unreasonable: but I think, only in being angry at my failure. A pupil from whom nothing is ever demanded which he cannot do, never does all he can. (20–21)

Discourse of this kind allowed Mill at last to feel his anger and at last to comprehend its sources. But even as (in a cautious and a measured manner) he finally expressed his indignation, he also demonstrated to his own satisfaction that his lifelong impressions of solitude and sorrow were essentially unfounded. Mill seems to have persuaded himself in these intricate, unconsciously strategic passages that James's apparent lack of regard and seemingly gratuitous aggressiveness could be interpreted as manifestations of the most tender paternal devotion. He seems to have convinced himself that he was abased and abused only because his father wanted him to accomplish "all he [could]." He acknowledges that his parent maimed him. However, he decided that "in the main his method was right," because it encouraged him to expect and to achieve "success." James's "method was right," Mill ultimately concludes, because it was motivated by a profound love and a beautiful hope for his child.

Mill's impulse simultaneously to accuse and to exonerate his father is especially evident and especially touching on those occasions when he discusses James's inability to display affection. "It must be mentioned," he remarks, ". . . that my father's children neither loved him, nor, with any warmth of affection, any one else." He comments that he "grew up in the absence of love & in the presence of fear" (*Early Draft*, 183–84). He observes that "the element which was chiefly lacking in [James's] moral relation to his children, was that of tenderness" (32). Mill never recants these, for himself, large and long-postponed realizations. But he does try to reduce their significance. He writes:

I do not mean that things were worse in this respect than they are in most English families; in which genuine affection is altogether exceptional. . . . I believe there is less personal affection in England than in any other country of which I know anything, & I give my father's family not as peculiar in this respect but only as a too faithful exemplification of the ordinary fact. (*Early Draft*, 183–84)

This analysis dissatisfied Mill: he revised the passage for publication. In the *Autobiography*'s final text he declares:

I do not believe that [my father's] deficiency lay in his own
nature. I believe him to have had much more feeling than he
habitually shewed, and much greater capacities of feeling
than were ever developed. He resembled most Englishmen in
being ashamed of the signs of feeling, and by the absence of
demonstration, starving the feelings themselves. If we consider
further that he was in the trying position of sole teacher, and
add to this that his temper was constitutionally irritable, it is
impossible not to feel pity for a father who did, and strove to
do, so much for his children, who would have valued their
affection, yet who must have been feeling that fear of him
was drying it up at its source. This was no longer the case,
later in life and with his younger children. They loved him
tenderly: and if I cannot say so much of myself, I was always
loyally devoted to him. (32)

In both versions of this material Mill at last recognizes that his father's love was incomplete and defective. He brings himself to believe, however, that the "deficiency" did not "lay in [his father's]
own nature" so much as in his father's cultural circumstances. He
convinces himself that his father had to be remote, "irritable," and
terrifying because he was English, and all Englishmen are "ashamed
of the signs of affection." [4] He even persuades himself that James's
inability to express "the signs of feeling" should be interpreted as an
indication of the profoundness of his feelings. It was, he declares,
because James was "in the trying position of sole teacher" that he
had to restrain his desire to shower his son with sympathy and affection. It was because he "did, and strove to do, so much" for his child
that, reluctantly and forcibly, he had to inhibit his tenderness. In
this context, Mill imagines, James's awful but involuntary coldness
should be understood as a manifestation of his unusually passionate
regard and respect. Mill goes so far as to assure himself that he
should view it as the sign of his special significance and favor that he
was made to labor and to learn rather than encouraged to love his
father "tenderly." It was, he persuades himself, because James felt so
much less for "his younger children" that he gave them mere pa-
tronizing affection rather than high expectations and rigorous, in-
vigorating reserve. Precisely because his father loved his eldest son
so much, he had no choice but to seem to love him very little. All

"true pity" in this truly pitiable situation should be directed, Mill concludes, not to himself but to the selfless parent who "would have valued [Mill's] affection" beyond all things, but who had to deny himself that deeply desired pleasure in order that he might give the child whom he most "devotedly" loved an environment in which he could fully develop his precocious abilities.

The stratagem is as bold as it is complex. Throughout the *Autobiography*, Mill tried to express and to cure the feelings of bewilderment, grief, disappointment, and fury which had afflicted him all his life. He reviewed and recorded his history primarily because he longed to defy and to deny it. Particularly he longed to persuade himself that he actually did receive from his father the love he craved but could never feel embracing and supporting him. Mill wrote the *Autobiography*, I am suggesting, less because he wanted to remember his experience than because he needed to reject and to revise it.[5]

An important element of his experience that Mill seems to have felt especially anxious to challenge and to change was the matter of his own and his father's relationship with his mother, Harriet Mill. One of the most peculiar and most fascinating circumstances about the *Autobiography* is the fact that Mill does not once mention his mother in the final draft of the work. In the first draft version of the book he refers to her on but nine occasions. Only once does he speak about her at any length.[6] In his entire lifetime, this is to say, Mill wrote but one sustained description of his mother. Even this passage is abbreviated. It contains but ninety-three words, and it is shocking in its repressed anger and antipathy. Mill remarks:

> That rarity in England, a really warm hearted mother, would
> in the first place have made my father a totally different
> being, & in the second would have made the children grow
> up loving and being loved. But my mother with the very
> best intentions, only knew how to pass her life in drudging
> for them. Whatever she could do for them she did, & they
> liked her, because she was kind to them, but to make herself
> loved, looked up to, or even obeyed, required qualities which
> she unfortunately did not possess. (*Early Draft*, 184)

Here and whenever Mill addresses the subject of his mother, he expresses abject contempt and dislike. He also expresses an urgent desire to deny both the fact of his mother's existence and the meaning of his father's involvement with her existence. Mill declares, for example, that his mother was "ill assorted" (*Early Draft,* 66) to his father. He insists that his father "had not, & never could have supposed that he had, the inducements of kindred intellect, tastes, or pursuits" (*Early Draft,* 36) when he decided to marry her. He observes that all his father's emotions about and reactions to his mother constituted "a conduct than which nothing could be more opposed, both as a matter of good sense and of duty, to the opinions which, at least at a later period of life, he strenuously upheld" (4). The mystification that Mill communicates in these remarks camouflages but does not conceal his almost consciously jealous determination to ignore and, if possible, to negate the sexuality of his parents' relationship. Mill seems to have found it excruciatingly difficult, even as an adult, to accept the fact that his father felt passionately attracted to his mother. Rather than allow himself to identify *the* reason why James should have wanted to have "married and had a large family," he forced himself to conclude that his parents' response to one another was incoherent and incomprehensible.

We are able to understand, as Mill could not, that his expressions of bewilderment masked a clear and an intensely painful comprehension of his father's conduct. We are able to understand that Mill's impulse to deny Harriet's claims upon James emanated from his continuing unconscious longing to invalidate those claims, and to himself assume the positions, functions, and roles from which he once had hoped to expel her. As we read these passages, we discover that Mill never wholly recovered from his Oedipal crisis. We recognize that the adult who wrote these professions of perplexity was the direct descendant of the child who subconsciously yearned to become not only his father's son, pupil, heir, and companion but also his formally acknowledged spousal mate.[7]

The content of all the language Mill ever wrote about his mother, and the startling fact that he wrote so little about her, together suggest that something even more active and more calculated than simple denial may have been controlling his responses. Mill well may have tried to use his reticence or forgetfulness to punish Harriet for winning that ultimate unification with his father which had been prohibited to himself. Nothing more completely could have conveyed anger and exacted revenge than this glaringly public absenting—this immense and symbolically brutal refusal to recognize any of Harriet's effects or influences upon his life. It even may be said that forbidding his mother access to the *Autobiography* metaphorically annihilated her. By ignoring her reality in the public representation of his own reality, Mill figuratively discreated Harriet. He seems to have satisfied the compelling demands of his lifelong primal rage by forgetting, destroying, or, to put no fine word upon the process, murdering his mother in the *Autobiography*.

The gratifications that Mill received from this metaphorical assassination probably had much to do with the symbology and the subliminalness of his behavior. He did not ever find it possible consciously to acknowledge how hurt and how furious his mother always had made him feel. Nor, of course, did he ever find it possible directly to rid himself of her: he could not consciously despise or literally kill her. Writing Harriet out of the record of his life seems to have allowed Mill to express his instinctively angry reaction, and yet to preserve the necessary subconsciousness of his reaction. The devices of his literature permitted him to carry out his will to kill without requiring him to recognize that he wanted to kill. Ostracizing his mother from the formal story of his life—expunging her, in effect, from her participation in his universe and from her place in his memory—probably gave Mill particular satisfaction because it was, as an action, violent *and* discreet, absolute *and* surreptitious.

Banishing his mother from the *Autobiography* almost certainly had for Mill another important retributive and consoling effect. Neglecting and denying the parent who, he believed, had neglected and denied him may have greatly lessened his consciousness of rejection and loss. By representing Harriet as an abominable nullity, Mill presumably reduced her power to cause him pain. His mother disregarded and abandoned him, he remembered. But, he seems to have thought, she was so insignificant a creature that her desertion can have no ultimate significance. He was better off without her, he implies, because she was in any case an absurd nonentity. In fact, he declares, she was a creature not even worth writing about.

This conception and its gratifications may well have extended to Mill's hurt and bewildered reaction to his parents' marriage. Asserting and, as it were, demonstrating Harriet's total insignificance probably had for Mill the effect of at last diminishing and perhaps even neutralizing his anguished sense of her importance to his father. As he subconsciously planned her ostracism from the *Autobiography,* he probably thought something like the following: My mother was a piece of triviality. Her place in my father's life, therefore, could not have been of much consequence. *I* was the only consequential person in my father's life.

Writing the *Autobiography* seems to have helped Mill finally to organize and finally to satisfy a number of his major subliminal needs. Writing the book apparently put at his disposal the power to recognize and the power not to recognize. His refusal to love, to describe, or even to acknowledge his mother seems to have permitted Mill to express and to avenge the unacceptable anger which he always had felt toward the woman who he believed had abandoned him and had stolen for herself the person whom he most loved and most needed. I am not contending that authoring the *Autobiography* cured Mill of his neuroses. I am suggesting that creating the *Autobiography* relieved many of the pressures that his neuroses always had mounted against Mill's mind; and that it did so by allowing the neuroses' material of confusion, mourning, and vindictive hatred to become articulated, symbolically acted upon, and yet ignored.

Mill orders the entire *Autobiography* upon this mechanism or strategy of simultaneously expressing and denying his most subversive and his most persistent instincts. Describing himself as a man who could at once experience and suppress everything volatile in his psychology seems to have given him a pleasing sense of authority over both his history and his imagination. This consoling conception gradually dominates the processes and the structures of his self-portraiture. It is one of Mill's principal purposes in the *Autobiography* to characterize himself as a creature who has no untoward, unruly, or ungovernable impulses. He represents himself in the book not as a personality replying to irresistible passions and percepts, but as an intelligence answering to disinterested wisdoms. He tries to describe himself as an essentially affectless and disembodied mind, an instrument for detached and formal speculation rather than an emotive individual who somewhat chaotically responds to unique and fractious desires, drives, and demands. In effect, and probably in subconscious intention, Mill at last fulfilled the mandate of his childhood in the *Autobiography.* He defines himself in his narrative as the minimally responsive, perfectly controlled, purely intellective being whom his father had insisted that he become.

Mill's impulse to desensitize his own personality may be observed everywhere in the *Autobiography*. We shall recall that he begins the work by declaring:

> It seems proper that I should prefix to the following bio-
> graphical sketch some mention of the reasons which have
> made me think it desirable that I should leave behind me
> such a memorial of so uneventful a life as mine. I do not for a
> moment imagine that any part of what I have to relate, can
> be interesting to the public as a narrative, or as being con-
> nected with myself. But I have thought that . . . it may be
> useful that there should be some record of an education
> which was unusual and remarkable. . . . It has also seemed
> to me that in an age of transition in opinions, there may be
> somewhat both of interest and of benefit in noting the suc-
> cessive phases of any mind which was always pressing for-
> ward, equally ready to learn and to unlearn either from its
> own thoughts or from those of others. But a motive which
> weighs more with me than either of these, is a desire to make
> acknowledgement of the debts which my intellectual and
> moral development owes to other persons. (3)

The passage expresses, and seems to *want* to express, an almost total failure of coenesthesia. Mill appears to have derived a powerful plea-sure from his unwillingness to identify his materiality and its con-ditions. He seems to have enjoyed refusing to recognize anything subrational or libidinal in the content and in the structure of his imagination. He happily indicates that everything which he can de-scribe as being "connected with [himself]" defines itself solely by mind, and by mind's means of knowing. He speaks of his entire sen-sibility as a bodying forth of absolutely conscious "opinions"; an ac-cretion of invariably clear and invariably precise "thoughts." He speaks of his mental activity as though it were an agency or an entity that is somehow discrete from himself: an "it" rather than an essen-tial portion of a large and various, often thoroughly sensual self-hood. When I earlier spoke of the *Autobiography*'s opening paragraph, I remarked that the material is fascinating because it reveals how difficult Mill always found it to discriminate himself from his cir-cumstances and his sources. I now suggest that this symbolic self-effacement ultimately became his choice as well as his fate. As he wrote the *Autobiography*, Mill seems to have grown finally and forever comfortable with the idea of himself as a wholly supraliminal, entirely indebted, completely impersonal intelligence. As he closed his career, he evidently enjoyed conceiving of himself as a man who experienced neither feelings nor needs, but only perfectly regulable values and views.

The paragraph I have cited is a characteristic performance. The lengths to which Mill goes in the *Autobiography* to conceal the fact and the nature of his sensuality are strange and sad (although, in an odd, inverse way they are very inventive). Mill almost never allows himself to refer in the book to his own primary personality. He cannot say: I felt, I sense, I grew, I became. He feels impelled to create such cold and clotted locutions as "It was at the period of my mental progress which I have now reached that . . ." (111). He almost never permits himself to describe his emotions as active, energetic, or unruled sensations. He cannot declare, for example, that he met, felt aroused by, fell in love with, wooed, and married a beautiful and wonderful woman named Harriet Taylor. He rather finds it necessary to write: "To be admitted into any degree of mental intercourse with a being of [her] qualities, could not help but have a most beneficial influence on my development; though the effect was only gradual, and many years elapsed before her mental progress and mine went forward, in the complete companionship they at last attained" (113). Throughout the *Autobiography*, Mill systematically obscures—or rejects—the fact that he was a passionate, affective, libidinal man. He denies the reality of his own existence almost as exorbitantly and almost as bellicosely as he denies the reality of his mother's existence.

Mill's obsessive dehumanization of himself eventually comes to seem the *Autobiography*'s secret theme or plot. We come to feel as intrigued and as moved by the remoteness and the antisensuality of Mill's prose as by the historicity of his tale. As we read and react to his deliberately dissociating language, we wonder what imaginative requirements he may have satisfied by submitting to this evidently urgent need to deprive himself of his own tangibleness. Why, we wonder, did Mill delight in repudiating his individuality? What pleasures did he win by repressing and effacing himself in his self-portrait?

The *Autobiography* and the life that produced the need to write it provide us with at least two answers to these questions. The first is perhaps the more obvious. It is likely that symbolically depersonalizing himself helped Mill acquire a final and lasting measure of control over the debilitating anxieties which his childhood had built into his consciousness. By convincing himself that he might be defined solely as his "intellectual and moral development," Mill appears at last to have invalidated, or at least to have diminished, the authority of his pain. He seems to have enjoyed refusing to be aware of himself as a man of feeling because this subconscious tactic released him from having to be consciously aware that what he always most deeply and most problematically felt was confusion, anger, and misery.

I believe it is primarily for this reason that the *Autobiography*'s prose is most fluent and most excited when it is least personal. This circumstance may perplex us. It may seem peculiar and even perverse that Mill can sound so happy when he represents himself in such impersonal and such inactive ways. But we are not Mill. For Mill, awareness of feeling must always have been awareness of suffering. His language becomes most quickened, skilled, and cheerful when he can avoid or reject the legitimacy of this awareness. His discourse sounds so content and even joyful when he conceals himself because denying his sensibility in his writing gave him the power to imagine that his "opinion," not his pain, and that his accomplishments, not his anguish, constituted his essence. When we encounter the *Autobiography* we encounter a most interesting and a most rare phenomenon. The book should be read, I think, as a work that extended to its author the ability to evade many of the pains and many of the pathologies that originally inspired his need to write it.

We can identify at least one other important reason why Mill found it necessary to dehumanize himself in his "biographical sketch." As I suggested earlier, it deeply gratified Mill to believe that the personality which he created in the *Autobiography* was much like the purely cerebral creature who had been his father's imaginative ideal. In his literature Mill figuratively transformed himself into the affectless creature whom he never quite could become in his life. While he described himself as solely a "mental life," he could feel that he actually had developed into the devitalized, almost completely ratiocinative son whom his father had expected him to become. The simulation was highly stimulating. By representing himself as a sexless mentality, Mill at last could experience the particular and precious ecstasy of pleasing his powerfully loved and powerfully loving parent.[8]

We may say more. The manners and the methods by which Mill defines himself in the *Autobiography*—his assertions, his language, his whole verbalized persona—all established him as a thoroughly dutiful son. At the same time, however, Mill insists that the uses to which he put this persona clearly demonstrate that he became an independent man. He was, he tells us, in every respect an obedient heir. But he always thought and wrote, he asserts, in such a way as to forge autonomous views and to forward sovereign ends. He declares, for example: "I thought for myself almost from the first, and occasionally thought differently from [my father], though for a long time only on minor points, and making his opinion the ultimate standard" (19). As he grew older, he observes, "[my] writings were no longer mere reproductions and applications of the doctrines I had been taught; they were original thinking . . .; and I do not exceed the truth in saying that there was a maturity, and a well-digested character about them" (72). Eventually, Mill suggests, he separated from his father. At the same time, though, he adored and clung to him. In an intricate and cautious paragraph, Mill writes:

> My father's tone of thought and feeling, I now felt myself at a
> great distance from: greater, indeed, than a full and calm
> explanation and reconsideration on both sides, might have
> shewn to exist in reality. . . . On those matters of opinion on
> which we differed, we talked little. He knew that the habit
> of thinking for myself, which his mode of education had fos-
> tered, sometimes led me to opinions different from his, and
> he perceived from time to time that I did not always tell him
> *how* different. I expected no good, but only pain to both of
> us, from discussing our differences: and I never expressed
> them but when he gave utterance to some opinion or feeling
> repugnant to mine, in a manner which would have made it
> disingenuousness on my part to remain silent. (108)

As he recreated and reevaluated his experiences in the *Autobiography*, Mill seems to have simultaneously yielded to and renounced his parent's emotional programme. In his psyche, he persuaded himself, he was a loyal and a loving son. In his work, he believed, he was a free agent; he was, indeed, the preeminent contemporary champion of individualism and liberty. His artful way of understanding and portraying himself seems to have permitted Mill to see himself at the end of his life as both his father's object and his own man. In writing the *Autobiography,* Mill at last found a means by which symbolically to unite his infantilism with his adulthood. He at last found a way to feel "at a great distance from" his parent while yet allowing that "distance" to be "never expressed."

This possibility helps explain the otherwise peculiar exuberance of the *Autobiography's* prose. I believe that the book's stark, self-concealing language seems so confident and so happy because Mill felt delight as he restructured or authored his history. He felt delight, I believe, because by writing his complicated and careful narrative he at last was satisfying and yet definitively escaping from his intimidating father. He felt delight, I believe, because he finally had created a scheme by which he might represent his lifelong submission to his parent as an imaginary "development" into creative individualism.

I have described the *Autobiography* as an extraordinarily self-effacing memoir. I have suggested that in his "biographical sketch" Mill unconsciously felt extremely reluctant to identify and to praise himself. This also was an important trait of his conscious thought. In both his public and his private literature he repeatedly proclaimed that excessive self-involvement (by which he often seems to have meant virtually any self-involvement) is reprehensible and ridiculous. To Florence Nightingale, for example, he wrote: "No earthly power can ever prevent the constant unceasing unsleeping elastic pressure of human egotism from weighing down and thrusting aside those who have not the power to resist it. Where there is life there is egotism."[9] This is a characteristic declaration. Throughout the final years of his career Mill spoke vigorously against the insipidity and the dangerousness of the "pressure of human egotism."

And yet, despite Mill's conscious and unconscious campaigns against egotism, and despite his many motives for depersonalizing himself in his own work, the *Autobiography* frequently assumes an aggressively self-assured and self-assertive tone. As we read the work we often encounter what seem to be congratulations or celebrations of self. The narrative is layered with passages that may strike us as especially egregious exhibitions of "the constant unceasing unsleeping elastic pressure of human egotism." What is startling and intriguing about these passages is the fact that they aggrandize not Mill himself, but his father and his wife. To our amusement—and, I think, to our sorrow—we discover that in the *Autobiography*, as so often in his life, Mill manifests a sensibility which focused an inordinate amount of attention and regard not upon his own but upon two other persons' egos.

Let us consider Mill's descriptions of his father. Early in the *Autobiography*, Mill panegyrizes his parent's achievements as an historian and as a statesman in terms that are shockingly extravagant; in terms which are almost consciously and certainly very strangely boastful. He writes:

> I still think [the *History of British India*], if not the most, one of the most instructive histories ever written, and one of the books from which most benefit may be derived by a mind in the course of making up its opinions. . . . And his dispatches, following his History, did more than ever had been done before to promote the improvement of India, and teach Indian officials to understand their business. If a selection of them were published, they would, I am convinced, place his character as a practical statesman fully on a level with his eminence as a speculative writer. (17)

He later remarks:

> I have never known any man who could do such ample justice to his best thoughts in colloquial discussion. His perfect command over his great mental resources, the terseness and expressiveness of his language and the moral earnestness as well as the intellectual force of his delivery, made him one of the most striking of all argumentative conversers. . . . It was not solely, or even chiefly, in diffusing his merely intellectual convictions, that his power shewed itself: it was still more through the influence of a quality, of which I have only since learnt to appreciate the extreme rarity: that exalted public

spirit and regard above all things to the good of the whole, which warmed into life and activity every germ of similar virtue that existed in the minds he came into contact with. (62)

Throughout the *Autobiography,* Mill eulogizes James's character and accomplishments with similar excitement and excessiveness. On almost every occasion that he refers to his father, he speaks with a peculiarly abandoned air of exultation, as though he felt somehow personally jubilant or triumphant on his parent's behalf.

Mill's extrusive or impersonal egotism is especially notable when he tries to demonstrate the pervasiveness of his father's influence. At one point in the *Autobiography* he insists that his father's sphere of authority in fact was pandemic. He declares:

My father's conversations and personal influence made his opinions tell on the world; cooperating with the effect of his writings in making him a power in the country, such as it has rarely been the lot of an individual in a private station to be, through the mere force of intellect and character: and a power which was often acting the most efficiently where it was least seen and suspected. . . . Much of what was done by Ricardo, Hume, and Grote, was the result, in part, of his prompting and persuasion. He was the good genius by the side of Brougham in most of what he did for the public, either on education, law reform, or any other subject. And his influence flowed in minor streams too numerous to be specified. (55–56)

He later observes:

The influence which Bentham exercised was by his writings. Through them he has produced, and is producing, effects on the condition of mankind, wider and deeper, no doubt, than any which can be attributed to my father. He is a much greater name in history. But . . . it was my father's opinions which gave the distinguishing character to the Benthamic or utilitarian propagandism of that time. (62)

Mill is asserting in these florid passages that his father was "the good genius" of all rational and public-spirited "life and activity" in the nineteenth-century "world." His parent's "influence" and "effects," he insists, "flowed" (63) everywhere. His "power," like God's, "was often acting the most efficiently where it was least seen and suspected." His father was the unpublicized but formative force behind the work of Ricardo, Hume, Grote, Brougham, and, as the *Autobiography* compulsively tries to demonstrate, J. S. Mill. "Benthamism" itself is a misnomer. The entire "Benthamic or utilitarian" era in the history of Western civilization should be known and celebrated, Mill contends, as the Age of James Mill.

Mill's responses to his wife in the *Autobiography* are even more hyperbolic than his responses to his father. This is especially true of his introductory description of Harriet. In an access of overwrought devotion, Mill writes:

> Alike in the highest regions of speculation and in the smallest
> practical concerns of daily life, her mind was the same perfect
> instrument, piercing to the very heart and marrow of the
> matter; always seizing the essential idea or principle. The
> same exactness and rapidity of operation, pervading as it did
> her sensitive as well as her mental faculties, would have fitted
> her to be a consummate artist, as her fiery and tender soul
> and her vigorous eloquence would certainly have made her a
> great orator, and her profound knowledge of human nature
> and discernment and sagacity in practical life, would in the
> times when such a *carriere* was open to women, have made
> her eminent among the rulers of mankind. (112–13)

As we observed earlier, Mill represents Harriet as the most intelligent, the most resourceful, and the most compassionate human being who ever has lived. He exclaims:

> Her intellectual gifts did but minister to a moral character at
> once the noblest and best balanced which I have ever met
> with in life. Her unselfishness was not that of a taught system of duties, but of a heart which thoroughly identified
> itself with the feelings of others, and often went to excess in
> consideration for them, by imaginatively investing their feel-

ings with the intensity of its own. The passion of justice might have been thought to be her strongest feeling, but for her boundless generosity, and a lovingness ever ready to pour itself forth upon any of all human beings who were capable of giving the smallest feeling in return. The rest of her moral characteristics were such as naturally accompany these qualities of mind and heart: the most genuine modesty combined with the loftiest pride; a simplicity and sincerity which were absolute, towards all who were fit to receive them; the utmost scorn for whatever was mean and cowardly, and a burning indignation at everything brutal or tyrannical, faithless or dishonorable in conduct and character. (113)

Like the passages which eulogize James, the *Autobiography*'s characterizations of Harriet are so extremely immoderate as to seem, despite their formal disinterestedness, vainglorious and vaunting. The subject of the writing is impersonal and projected. But in the detached and symbolic senses that Mill evidently required, the writing is egotistical. In his "biographical sketch" as in his life, Mill apparently could situate and value himself only by extravagantly magnifying the significance of the only two persons in the world whom he ever felt able to love.

To perceive this circumstance is not at once to comprehend its meanings. As we read the *Autobiography*, few other questions more interest and more confound us than the question of what ground Mill found for himself in the story of his own life. How and for what reason, we wonder, did he derive personal satisfaction from writing encomia to James and to Harriet? In what respects could he identify and assert his own personality in a work which seems almost exclusively aware of and almost exclusively excited by other persons' personalities?

The answers to these questions are contained, I believe, in the history which the *Autobiography* records and to which it reacts. In the *Autobiography*, Mill makes it clear that his childhood experience deprived him of almost all the cognitions and certitudes that permit a man to develop a strong and a spontaneous ego identity.[10] The passages we have examined make it clear that, even during the final years of his life, most of Mill's energy, intelligence, and creativity had to be set aside to invent and to articulate the mental image not of himself, but of his sire and his spouse. As we have seen, Mill eventually developed a full complement of psychical constituents: like other men, he experienced excitations, tensions, drives, and desires. Apparently, however, he could define and accept his own sensations and urges only by regarding them as the overflow or the gifts of his more powerful sponsors. He seems to have been able to vent "the constant unceasing unsleeping elastic pressure" of *his* egotism only by trivializing himself and aggrandizing his father and his wife. The *Autobiography* indicates that for Mill intuitive and innate ego-identification was, in the language of psychoanalysis, ego-dystonic. Ego-identification felt toward and expressed on behalf of his two ego-ideals was ego-syntonic.[11]

To ourselves this situation may seem tragic or possibly even comic. We cannot readily imagine how any man could regard an identification based upon two vast subordinations as anything other than an impossibly humiliating infringement of selfhood, liberty, and life itself. We learn from the *Autobiography,* however, that an identity built even upon his emasculated role as his father's and his wife's psychological vassal seemed to Mill incomparably more stable and more satisfying than no identity at all. The fact that his history was awful and the fact that the self-image which his history produced was morbidly dependent appears not to have consciously disturbed him. To discover that in the course of living his extremely difficult life he had acquired a specific and a persisting personality was in itself an exciting experience for Mill. The personality he developed was passive, subordinate, and perhaps enslaved. But it was also authentic and individual: his own and no one else's. I am suggesting that recording the history of his pathologically dependent "mental life" helped Mill realize that he had a mental life. Describing his excessively submissive character helped him realize that he had a character. He was the person, Mill learned and asserted, who was the cherished son of an almighty Father. He was the person who was the treasured husband of an all-important Wife. He was the person who was important because he was intimately involved with two great world-historical genuises.

This is one of the major reasons, I believe, that Mill's prose becomes so excited and even, as I have put it, so egotistical when he eulogizes his father and his wife. Although he technically refers in these passages to other persons' achievements, virtues, and strengths, it apparently felt to him that he was celebrating his own accomplishments and significance. In the *Autobiography* as in his subconscious psychology, Mill seems to have identified himself as the sum of his affiliations and his subserviences. He experienced, it seems, an odd, exteriorized narcissism. The elation with which he defined and glorified his dependencies testifies to the joy and the pride that he derived from feeling himself able at last to claim any kind of identification—even a tragic, an absurd, or a comic identification.

I believe that we can identify at least one other reason for Mill's excitement in the *Autobiography*. Early in the text Mill declares that "the question 'Who made me?' cannot be answered, because we have no experience or authentic information from which to answer it" (27). One of the sources of Mill's agitation and happiness in the *Autobiography* undoubtedly was that writing about his life provided him with enough "authentic information" to answer this fundamental question; and to answer it in a manner that surprised and fulfilled him. The "information" he gained by remembering and by reordering his history taught him that, although his father, his wife, and his civilization all had contributed to his "intellectual and moral development," Mill himself ultimately "made" Mill. In the *Autobiography*, Mill makes it evident that he neither chose nor ever completely enjoyed his experience. He makes it equally apparent, however, that he did create and relish the consciousness which his experience stimulated, the consciousness which finally came to constitute his sensibility.

By telling the story of his "mental progress," Mill discovered that his percepts comprised an "authentic information." And he discovered that the meaning of this "information" was himself. As he contemplated the whole prospect or field of his life, Mill at last consciously realized that it was he himself who had developed the impressions, the ideas, the visions, and the values which had made him a presence in the world and a subject for an autobiography. He knew that his psychology was not sovereign. He knew that he was irreducibly linked to his father, to his mother, and to his wife. But he recognized that he himself had forged those chains; and he recognized, at last, that he had made himself a distinctive and an extraordinarily productive person by doing so. Mill is an excited writer in the *Autobiography* because as he wrote the work—as he composed an entire book concerned solely with the subject of himself—he con-

sciously perceived that he was describing and feeling the indestructi-
ble pleasures of a fully defined and a fully accepted personality.

The *Autobiography* does not permit either its author or its audience
to romanticize the personality that Mill "made." The narrative continually reveals that the character which he constructed was com-
pliant, menial, and even, in some respects, servile. I have suggested
that this seemed to Mill himself a much less significant circumstance than another fact which the work demonstrates to be true, the
fact that his dependencies and his debilities ultimately were resources, because they constituted a substance and an identity. Much
of the "authentic information" that Mill assembled about himself is
extremely disturbing. But the material also is coherent, unified,
unique, and of Mill's own devising. I believe it is primarily for this
reason that, despite the often dismaying nature of the "information"
it communicates, the *Autobiography*'s tone is remarkably confident
and happy. The *Autobiography* is a strong and a stimulating book because its author proved to himself by writing it that he was a strong
and a stimulating man.

I have tried to explain why Mill believed that he had to organize
his discussion of this most personal of subjects, the subject of himself, in seemingly impersonal ways. I have tried to show how remoteness moves into intimacy in the *Autobiography*; and how dis-
passion, or even coldness, converts itself into passion in the book. I
have tried to demonstrate that this collision between and eventual
intersection of detachment and engagement is crucial to Mill's purposes in the *Autobiography* and crucial to our own interest in the
work. I have tried to point out that for both author and audience the
matter of principal significance in the *Autobiography* is the manner in
which an impulse to desensitize a self gradually evolves into an impulse to acknowledge, to enjoy, and to assert a self.

Many people find Mill's literature deficient in its feelings and
sparse in its excitements. The *Autobiography* seems to some readers
the least engaging of the major works of modern autobiography. I do
not share these views. I believe that the *Autobiography* is a profoundly
moving and a profoundly important achievement. Sometimes Mill's
writing seems stiff and contorted. His attitudes occasionally may appear to be wary or defensive. But the emotions that the *Autobiography* examines and resolves are extraordinarily interesting, and of
volcanic intensity. No doubt Mill's cognitions and beliefs are less

striking and less beautiful than, for example, Wordsworth's. Certainly Mill was less ardently involved with himself and less clairvoyantly aware of himself than Rousseau. The *Autobiography* seems to me, however, fully as inventive and at least as significant a creation as *The Prelude* or *The Confessions*. For Mill shares, I believe, Wordsworth's and Rousseau's great impulse: the impulse to claim an identification; the impulse to locate and to seize a definitive, a durable, and a describable character.

Mill's impulse and his power to fulfill it seem particularly impressive when we take into account the terrible wounds he suffered during his infancy and youth. As we read about and as we react to his experience, how can we help but consider it almost miraculous that a person so damaged could develop so determined a desire to rescue himself from extermination? As we have seen, the injuries Mill suffered were of such severity that they permanently affected his ability to feel and his ability to communicate. But we must not allow ourselves to be misled by or to be impatient with the symptoms of his illnesses. I have hoped to demonstrate that in this, his most emotional and his most expressive work, Mill's verbal and affective convolutions may be unraveled. We may see through his inhibitions, anxieties, and disguises. We may find in the text of the *Autobiography* that which Mill himself seems to have discovered in writing the book: the presence of a living being; the testimony of a person who was grievously troubled, but who also was indomitably resilient and indefatigably creative.

*—This must be, & may be borne
with, when one's own path is clear—
and mine is always becoming clearer.*

———————————7

"One's Own Path Is Clear"

I have suggested that Mill
wrote literature primarily because he needed to reorder or, as he put
it, to "make [his] own character." I have tried to demonstrate that as
a philospher and as an artist the principal impulse to which he responded was his desire to construct a power to feel and a power to
communicate. Mill believed that he ultimately accomplished this
difficult task. He believed that in the process of creating his seemingly impersonal discourse he gradually won for himself a state of
consciousness which his history had threatened to deny to him, a
consciousness that he possessed an organic, sensual connection with
other people, with the natural universe, and with his own experience.

Mill could not "make" an entirely new psychology. Until the end
of his life he had to contend with the horrifying instinction that all
his substance and all his worth inhered in his art. He always believed
that he was grotesquely inept in the common affairs of daily life. He
always feared that he was insufficiently sensual. He always thought
that he was essentially unlikable. Mill almost never spoke in a direct
way about his pain. But melancholy and misgiving frequently seem

to lift off his prose, and to surround his thought like a sorrowful glimmer or glow. Characteristic of this effect is a letter Mill wrote late in his life to F. D. Maurice. In a mood of extreme loneliness and grief, he declares:

> I sympathize with the feeling of (if I may call it so) mental loneliness which shows itself in your letter & sometimes in your published writings. In our age & country, every person with any mental power at all, who both thinks for himself & has a conscience, must feel himself, to a very great degree alone. I should think you have decidedly more people who are in real connection with you than I have. I am in this supremely happy, that I have had, & even now have, that communion in the fullest degree where it is most valuable of all, in my home. But I have it nowhere else; & if people did but know how much more precious to me is the faintest approach to it, than all the noisy eulogiums in the world!¹

As we have seen, this feeling of aloneness, this sense of scarcely expressible sadness, always had haunted Mill. As early as 1834 he had written:

> Every increase of insight carries with it the uncomfortable feeling of being separated more & more widely from *almost* all other human beings. . . . One feels more & more that one is drifting so far out of the course of other men's navigation as to be altogether below their horizon; not only that they will not go with us, but they cannot see whither we are steering, & believe if ever they catch a glimpse of us, that we are letting ourselves go blindly whither we may. However this must be, & may be borne with, when one's own path is clear—and mine is always becoming clearer.²

Mill made a brave and a fascinating attempt to rebuild his sensibility. But the griefs, injuries, and losses that his experience had imposed upon him had been terrible in their force and in their cost. In his work as a writer Mill changed much about his character and his consciousness. Throughout his life, however, he suffered gravely from his unconquerable feeling of "mental loneliness."

And yet, despite the fact that Mill always felt isolated and sorrowful, he never succumbed to these emotions. His fears and his frustrations afflicted his life. But he never surrendered to his anxieties. Mill could not make himself completely confident or completely happy. But he did learn to accept and to explore his extraordinary "mental power" and his exemplary "conscience." And he learned to do this in such a way as to become of inestimable service to his wife, to his family, to his society, and to his civilization.

We may say more. On a number of occasions Mill remarked that the "character" he "made" by writing his cautious and continent literature seemed to himself unexpectedly substantial and satisfying. Readers who are sympathetic to the man and to the nature of his suffering will recognize the excitement and the hopefulness that charge his declarations of this kind. His senses of sufficiency and exaltation are especially evident in a letter he wrote to Carlyle. In the intimacy and the trust of what was at the time a strong friendship, Mill exclaimed:

> I [have] come into a more settled state. I think that I have obtained something like a firm footing, and additional rather than new light; I can hardly say that I have changed any of my opinions, but I seem to myself to *know* more, from increased experience of my own feelings. All which is thus acquired *must* be clear gain; it is increased knowledge of *Realities;* and it must be for want of will if with additional ground to build upon, I cannot raise my edifice of Thought to a greater height and so look round and see more of Truth than I could see before.[3]

Mill's faith in his power "to see more of Truth" never became absolute. But it became considerable. Mill gradually realized that, like all his other, more abstractive subjects, his own sensibility could be made to become coextensive with his ability to describe it. He discovered that by transforming his fearsome history and his tortured "feelings" into the carefully neutralized material of his literature, he could "raise" a personality whose architecture was impregnably solid and unmistakably authentic.

Throughout his career, Mill frequently indicated that he thought of his literature *as* his experience. He repeatedly suggested that he regarded his discourse as the substance and as the voice of the man whom he wanted to be. Mill's attempt to convert himself into an "edifice of Thought" may seem to ourselves impracticable and perverse. But our reaction scarcely matters. The only person who had to live Mill's life believed that by literalizing his desperately conflicted consciousness he could equip himself to feel "more settled," more "firm," and almost infinitely capable of learning, labor, life, and love. In what I have been describing as the subliminal and the strategic aspects of its programme, the art that he created seemed to the artist himself to be triumphantly successful.

Mill's achievement may interest us in itself, as the triumph of a unique and a most admirable man. His achievement also may engage us for another reason. In Mill's life we may see, I believe, a triumph of reason and of character. We may see a victory of mind over mindlessness, and of will over circumstances. As we confront the literature and the life of J. S. Mill, we encounter heroism and a potential example. We find a demonstration that the love of individualism and the desire to develop an individuated experience cannot be exterminated—not if one can be as courageous, as intelligent, and as determined a man as John Mill.

Mill's life and literature teach us that disease may be converted into health. Disorder and despair may be transformed—or displaced—into insight, ingenuity, and capability. Pathology may be made to become creative. Mill's childhood was grotesque, and it probably should have crippled his character. He should have become, we may say, pinched, petty, narcissistic, and cruel. Mill became none of these things. He became, rather, inquisitive, generous, affectionate, conciliatory, inventive, and hopeful. His experience should have caused him to abominate society and socialization. Yet Mill cherished civilization, and he loved those modes of being that he believed civilization in its ideal forms could encourage and perhaps even confer. Everything in his early life conspired to afflict and to inhibit his personality. As an adult, though, Mill came to demand as his preference and as his right the power to identify himself and the ability to approve of himself. He developed a passionate faith in individualism, and a genius for describing both its essentialness and its imperilment. Mill's boyhood and youth could have forced him to loathe mind and to fear its mechanisms. But he treasured the methods and the experience of reasoning: no other person did more during the nineteenth century to advance the causes and to improve the quality of "intellectual culture" in England.

Mill accomplished all this because he wanted to. He so much desired and so much needed to become a free, a rational, a distinctive, and a loving man that he "made" himself into a person whom the conditions of his life would seem to have prohibited him from ever becoming. This, I believe, will prove to be Mill's final claim upon history. We always shall study Mill as an economist, a political scientist, a sociologist, a critic, and a philosopher. I believe, however, that we eventually shall wish to remember Mill as a hero of the human spirit. We shall wish to remember John Stuart Mill as a man who demanded and as a man who won the power to be sane, the power to be independent, the power to be intelligent, and the power to love.

NOTES

Introduction

    1. Norman O. Brown, *Life Against Death*, p. 183.

Chapter One: The Childhood

    1. Quoted by A. J. Mill in "The Education of John—Some Further Evidence," p. 11.

    2. James Mill experienced other, more conscious motivations: the philosophy of education was one of his principal professional interests. The *Analysis of the Human Mind* and his essay on "Education" for the *Encyclopedia Britannica* define the conscious convictions and hopes upon which he based his son's education. For an extensive and an excellent discussion of James Mill's less conscious concerns, see Bruce Mazlish, *James and John Stuart Mill.*

    3. J. S. Mill, *Autobiography and Other Writings,* p. 5. All subsequent references to the *Autobiography* will be to this edition. Page references will be provided in parentheses following the material cited.

    4. At a later point in my essay I shall speak to the question of why the *Autobiography*'s language is so cautious and quietistic.

5. J. S. Mill, *The Early Draft of John Stuart Mill's "Autobiography,"* pp. 179—80. All subsequent references to this work will be to *Early Draft*. Page references will be provided in parentheses following the material cited.

6. For particularly interesting material of this kind, see *Autobiography,* pp. 5, 13, 14, 20, 32—34.

7. It is a most significant circumstance that Mill allowed his wife to delete from the final draft of the *Autobiography* both of the passages I have cited above. Even as an adult, Mill evidently could not permit himself to liberate any conscious expressions of anger toward his father. At a later point in the essay I shall discuss this phenomenon.

8. Quoted in Michael St. John Packe, *The Life of John Stuart Mill* (1970), p. 76.

9. Quoted in Bertrand Russell and Patricia Russell, eds., *The Amberley Papers,* 1: 421.

10. Quoted in F. A. Hayek, *John Stuart Mill and Harriet Taylor: Their Correspondence and Subsequent Marriage,* p. 286n.

11. I shall more closely examine Mill's ways of writing about his mother in my discussion of the *Autobiography*.

12. For a more comprehensive discussion of these processes and of the principles that shape them, see Margaret S. Mahler et al., *The Psychological Birth of the Human Infant.* The work contains an extensive bibliography on the subject.

13. Apparently this phenomenon was somewhat common in the families of males who became significant writers during the Victorian era. A number of other important Victorian authors suggest in their autobiographical literature that they fulfilled intensely frustrating, excessively symbolic roles in their parents' marriages. In particular, Carlyle, Ruskin, Dickens, Thackeray, and Trollope seem to have suffered from having become the focus, or the cathexis, of their parents' most compulsive emotions. Unquestionably, however, Mill's situation was unique in its extremity and its effects. In a forthcoming book I shall discuss what appears to me to be a close, perhaps a formative relationship in the Victorian civilization between deeply disordered childhood experience and highly inventive adult creativity.

14. Sigmund Freud, *An Outline of Psychoanalysis,* p. 46.

15. For an extended discussion of the theory of the Oedipus complex, see Freud, *The Ego and the Id,* pp. 18—19. Freud gives his fullest and his most disturbing analysis of the "frightening end" which befalls the Oedipal hysteria in *Civilization and Its Discontents.* Mahler summarizes contemporary theories about the Oedipus complex in *The Psycho-*

logical Birth of the Human Infant. An interesting treatment of the subject may be found in Janet Malcolm, *Psychoanalysis: The Impossible Profession.*

16. See L. Hinsie and R. J. Campbell, eds., *Psychiatric Dictionary,* p. 521.

17. It became a matter of both great pride and great pain to Mill that his father required him to supervise his younger siblings' education. We are able to understand that James took this step because he needed to husband his time and energy. John, however, could only have supposed that his father meant more or less publicly to establish him as his colleague or as his partner—as, indeed, his spouse. Too, John undoubtedly supposed that James intended to make over to him certain of his own prerogatives: that he intended to define his son as a surrogate for himself. In these respects his duties delighted him. But his duties also threatened him. For during those hours in which he taught his brother and sisters he had to absent himself from his father. And by teaching his siblings he was conferring upon his rivals—he was conferring upon the very symbolizations of his inability to seduce and marry James—the substance of his own authority and identity.

It should be noted that John's siblings regarded their monitor-brother as a profoundly gentle and lovable substitute for their intimidating father. In their correspondence Mill's sisters repeatedly refer to John and his tutelage in the most admiring, grateful, and affectionate terms. It is a tribute to Mill that he found it possible to accomplish what was for himself an extremely painful obligation in such a way as to excite the loving esteem of the children whom he subliminally feared and resented.

18. It is highly significant that this subconscious rebellion took place solely on the physical plane. To have refused to develop intellectually should have been to have made an overt resistance to James. I have tried to suggest that Mill did not believe he could afford to make a conscious, tangible insurrection against his father.

19. J. S. Mill, *The Earlier Letters of John Stuart Mill, 1812—1848,* ed. F. B. Mineka (Toronto, 1963) in *The Collected Works of John Stuart Mill,* 12: 144. All subsequent references to this work will be to *EL.*

20. The fervency of Mill's impulse to incorporate himself with his father also may be observed in his description of his first formal employment. In the *Autobiography* he wrote: "In May 1823, my professional occupation and status for the next thirty-five years of my life, were decided by my father's obtaining for me an appointment from the East India Company, in the office of the Examiner of India Correspondence, immediately under himself" (pp. 50—51). The peculiarly happy tone of this oddly passive language has to do, we may imagine,

with Mill's pleasure in becoming in his "professional occupation and status," as in his writing and his intrapsychical consciousness, "immediately under" his father and "immediately" engaged in his father's pursuits. In this context, the phrase "immediately under" carries a distinctly sexual connotation.

21. At another point in the *Autobiography,* Mill declares that he "gradually, but completely recovered from [his] mental depression, and was never again subject to it" (p. 90). In fact he experienced a long series of depressive "maladies." It does seem to have been true, however, that the succeeding attacks or "relapses" were significantly less intense and prolonged than the "mental crisis" of 1826–27.

22. A. W. Levi, "The 'Mental Crisis' of John Stuart Mill." See also Mazlish, pp. 205–30.

23. In one of his most interesting letters, Mill indicates that he felt a kind of gratitude toward his depression. In 1833, while suffering from another attack of listlessness and despair, he wrote to Carlyle: "I will not if I can help it give way to gloom and morbid despondency, of which I have had a large share in my short life, and to which I have been indebted for all the most valuable of such insights as I have into the most important matters, neither will this return of it be without similar fruits, as I hope and almost believe" (*EL,* 12: 149).

24. Mill associates "the anti-self-consciousness theory" with Carlyle. In fact, though, he learned the "theory" from his father. His father, we recall, repeatedly and insistently instructed Mill in the necessity and in the uses of self-abnegation.

Chapter Two: Separation and Integration

1. I shall discuss Mill's relationship with Harriet Taylor in a later chapter.

2. Mill, *EL,* 12: 162.

3. Ibid., p. 154.

4. Ibid., p. 176.

5. Ibid., p. 204.

6. Ibid., p. 224.

7. Ibid., p. 157.

8. Mill, "The Spirit of the Age," in *Essays on Politics and Culture.* All subsequent references to "The Spirit of the Age" will be to this edition. Page references will be provided in parentheses following the material cited.

9. Mill, *EL,* 12: 455. In the contexts which I have been develop-

ing, Mill's parenthesis—"(quite independent of personal affection)"—obviously is of considerable significance.

10. For a discussion of Mill's identification-reaction, see Mazlish, pp. 212, 229.

11. Quoted in J. A. Froude, *Thomas Carlyle: A History of His Life in London, 1834–1881*, 1: 78–79.

12. Mill, *EL*, 12: 312.

13. Mill, "Civilization," in *Essays on Politics and Culture*, pp. 51, 52. All future references to "Civilization" will be to this edition. Page references will be provided in parentheses following the material cited.

14. Mill, "Bentham," in *Essays on Politics and Culture*, p. 87. All future references to "Bentham" will be to this edition. Page references will be provided in parentheses following the material cited.

15. Mill, *Autobiography*, p. 62. I shall discuss this passage at some length in my chapter on the *Autobiography*.

16. We shall recall that in 1836 Mill had told Lytton Bulwer that he meant to make it the principal concern of his career "to soften the harder and sterner features of [his father's] Radicalism and Utilitarianism."

17. Mill, "Coleridge," in *Essays on Politics and Culture*, p. 133. All future references to "Coleridge" will be to this edition. Page references will be provided in parentheses following the material cited.

18. Particularly Mill disagreed with Coleridge's defining belief that "the human mind [has] a capacity, within certain limits, of perceiving the nature and properties of 'Things in themselves'" (p. 140). Mill believed, like his father, that "there can be no ground for believing that anything can be the object of our knowledge except our experience, and what can be inferred from our experience by the analogies of experience itself" (p. 143). Mill agreed with his parent that there can be no "idea, feeling, power in the human mind, which, in order to account for it, requires that its origin should be referred to any other source" (p. 144). Mill's differences of *opinion* with Coleridge were elemental and absolute.

19. For a provocative discussion of Mill's analysis, see Raymond Williams, *Culture and Society*, pp. 49–70.

Chapter Three: Love and Marriage

1. For a full account of Harriet and Mill's relationship, see Hayek, *John Stuart Mill and Harriet Taylor*.

2. Mill, *The Later Letters of John Stuart Mill, 1849–1873*, ed. F. B. Mineka and D. N. Lindley (Toronto, 1972) in *The Collected Works of John*

Stuart Mill, 14: 42–43. All subsequent references to this work will be to *LL.*

3. Ibid., p. 166.

4. Ibid., 15: 615.

5. Quoted in Hayek, p. 14.

6. It is difficult to determine if Harriet warranted the esteem that Mill gave her. Several of Mill's biographers cast aspersions upon Harriet's abilities and even upon her motives. Other commentators seem, for more or less political reasons, to insist without documentation upon Harriet's genius and sanctitude.

We know distressingly little about Harriet Mill. What we do know about her seems to me at least in certain ways to confirm Mill's assessment of her character and her talents. Harriet was a remarkably gifted thinker, a deeply compassionate person, and a most tender lover. It seems clear, however, that Mill vastly underestimated his own importance in their intellectual association. His was the major mind in their marriage. At a later point in the essay, I shall attempt to identify some of the reasons why it may have excited Mill to exaggerate his wife's contributions to his life and to his work.

We need a full-scale biography of Harriet Mill. She was an exceptional woman whose history is of great interest and importance.

7. Mill, *EL,* 12: 184.

8. Mill, *Diary* (1854), quoted in Mill, *The Letters of John Stuart Mill,* 2: 361.

9. Mill, *Diary,* quoted ibid., p. 373.

10. Mill, *LL,* 14: 109.

11. Ibid., p. 126.

12. Ibid., p. 223.

13. Ibid., p. 11.

14. Ibid., p. 26.

15. Ibid., p. 112. This association of Harriet with Bentham completes the complicated circle of Mill's subconscious identifications. In chapter 2 we saw how closely Mill connected Bentham with "the late Mr. Mill." Here, as he unites Harriet with Bentham, Mill unconsciously is recognizing that he has reacted to his wife as a surrogate for his parent. No wonder he blesses her. Harriet is fulfilling for Mill a major and an otherwise unattainable need.

16. Mill, *LL,* 14: 250.

17. Ibid., p. 253.

18. Ibid., pp. 268, 274, 284.

19. Ibid., p. 4.

20. Ibid., p. 110.

21. Mill, *Diary* (1854), quoted in Elliot, 2: 357.

22. Mill, *LL,* 4: 373.

23. One of Mill's biographers has observed that "in Mill's unconscious, Harriet was . . . his mother as a desired Oedipal object. She
was also his mother as maternal figure. Everyone has noticed Mill's dependency on her in practical and household affairs . . . and how he
constantly noted down for Harriet the symptoms of his illnesses, as if
he were a child with its mother" (Packe, p. 286; see, too, Mazlish, pp.
283–88). I have tried to suggest that Harriet appealed so strongly to
Mill because he subconsciously regarded her as a version of his father—
a version whom, without either guilt or guile, he could sexualize and
love. I believe that the particular configurations of Mill's Oedipal hysteria required him to unite with a paternal rather than with a maternal
love object.

However, I have no wish to minimize the significance of the fact that
Mill found a wife who bore his mother's name and who fulfilled for him
many of the roles which normally are discharged for a man by his
mother. That his wife so efficiently amalgamated the symbolic properties of both his parents undoubtedly intensified Mill's neurotic identification and ardent overreaction.

24. Professor Mazlish believes that Mill "probably had no experience of sexual intercourse in his life" (p. 531). Mill's friend Alexander
Bain reported: "I am not singular in the opinion that in the so-called
sensual feelings, [Mill] was below average; that, in fact, he was not
a good representative specimen of humanity in respect of these; and
scarcely did justice to them in his theories. He was not an ascetic in any
sense; he desired that every genuine susceptibility to pleasure should be
turned to account, so far as it did not interefere with better pleasures;
but he made light of the difficulty of controlling the sexual appetite"
(Bain, *John Stuart Mill, A Criticism,* p. 149).

25. Mill, *LL,* 14: 256.

26. Ibid., p. 298.

27. Ibid., p. 259.

28. Ibid., 12: 521. Mill is completing an arc here. Throughout his
youth he often had believed that his father regarded him as a text. I
shall discuss this perception and its consequences for Mill in my chapter on the *Autobiography.*

29. Mill, *LL,* 14: 112.

30. Ibid., pp. 141–42.

31. Ibid., p. 168.

32. Ibid., p. 197.

33. Ibid., pp. 254–55.

34. Ibid., p. 165.
35. Ibid., p. 82.
36. Harriet's letters to Mill express this consciousness of mutuality with almost equal intensity and excitement. For representative expressions of her feelings of oneness with her husband, see Hayek, pp. 95, 96, 99.
37. Mill, *LL,* 14: 116.
38. Ibid., p. 47.
39. Mill, *Diary* (1844), quoted in Elliot, 2: 371.
40. Mill, *LL,* 15: 574.
41. Ibid., p. 622.
42. Bain, p. 102.
43. Mill, *LL,* 15:577
44. Earlier I suggested that throughout the years of their courtship and marriage, Harriet and Mill had invested the act of writing with symbolic sexual significance. I suggested that authoring texts probably became for them a substitute for sensual union—perhaps the only mode of intercourse that they ever allowed themselves. In this context, Mill perhaps should be understood as symbolically perpetuating his marriage with Harriet by continuing to write literature after her death. Probably his work unconsciously stimulated him to recover a very full sense of his wife's continuing presence and persisting love. We may hope so. This should have been a harmless happiness for an often acutely unhappy man.

Chapter Four: Resolution and Independence

1. Mill, *Principles of Political Economy,* 2 vols. (Toronto, 1965), in *The Collected Works of John Stuart Mill,* 2: 443–44.
2. Mill expresses this idea throughout his correspondence. In 1861, for example, he wrote to Henry Taylor: "Whenever the movement for organic change recovers strength, which may happen at any time, and is sure to happen at some time, it will make a great deal of practical difference what general theories of constitutional government are then in possession of the minds of cultivated persons. It is as a preparation for that time that my speculations . . . may be valuable. . . . If my opinions make any way, they will influence, more or less, what is done from time to time in the way of practical improvement; and while changes in the right direction will be facilitated, the barriers will, I hope, be strengthened against those of a bad tendency" (Mill, *LL,* 15: 731). In "Bentham," we recall, Mill remarks: "Speculative philosphy,

which to the superficial appears a thing so remote from the business of life and the outward interests of men, is in reality the thing on earth which most influences them, and in the long run overbears every other influence save those which it must itself obey" (Mill, "Bentham," p. 85).

3. Mill, *A System of Logic* (New York, 1869), p. 524.

4. Mill, *Principles of Political Economy*, 2: 451.

5. Mill, *Diary*, quoted in *Mill's Essays on Literature and Society*, p. 351.

6. Mill, *LL*, 16: 1380.

7. Ibid., 14: 294.

8. Ibid., p. 332. These passages help us realize that probably it was Mill who conceived of and who principally executed the works which he later attributed primarily to Harriet.

9. Mill, *On Liberty*, p. 3. All subsequent references will be provided in parentheses following the material cited.

10. Another commentator has interpreted the genesis and the utility of *On Liberty* in a quite different way. Howard R. Wolf remarks: "We can look to Mill's 'On Liberty' as a work in which he found compensation for years of submission by giving expression to the need to give 'full freedom to human nature to expand itself in innumerable and conflicting directions.' A political vision of freedom, valid in itself, was for Mill the working out of a neurotic conflict. Mill expressed in political philosophy the need for a freely chosen identity which had been denied him in his own childhood" (Wolf, "British Fathers and Sons, 1773–1913: From Filial Submissiveness to Creativity," p. 59). My views accord more closely with those of Mazlish, who observes: "[Mill's] own generational experience motivates and supplies the passion behind his abstract political discussion. The true psychology underlying Mill's political philosophy is his own life experience" (p. 398). Mill himself, as we shall see in chapter 5, believed that *On Liberty* was an accomplished work because it received more attention from his wife than any other of his creations.

Chapter Five: *"Language and Manner"*

1. Mill, *LL*, 14: 384.

2. Mill, *EL*, 12: 97.

3. Ibid., 13: 246.

4. Mill, *LL*, 14:373.

5. Ibid., 15: 704.

6. Ibid., 14: 313.

7. Ibid., 15: 678.

8. Ibid., p. 675.

9. Mill's ideas about "ascendancy" were not always so absolute—or so personal. In 1842 he wrote to R. B. Fox: "It is becoming more & more clearly evident to me that the moral regeneration of Europe must precede its social regeneration & also that none of the ways in which that mental regeneration is sought, Bible Societies, Tract Societies, Puseyism, Socialism, Chartism, Benthamism, &c. will *do,* though doubtless they all have some good elements of truth and good in them. I find quite enough to do in trying to make up my own mind as to the course which must be taken by the present great transitional movement of opinion & society. . . . In the meantime, I do not know that there is anything better for me to do than write the [works] I have been writing, destined to do [their] little part towards straightening & strengthening the intellects which have this great work to do" (Mill, *EL,* 13: 563–64).

10. Ibid., p. 474.

11. Ibid., 12: 163.

12. Ibid., p. 219.

13. Ibid., pp. 78–79.

14. Ibid., p. 222.

15. See Packe, pp. 369–70, 409, 477.

Chapter Six: 'Who Made Me?'

1. Because I have referred to the *Autobiography* throughout this essay, I shall restrict my attention for the most part in the chapter that follows to material from the text not previously discussed.

2. Charles Dickens, *David Copperfield,* ed. G. H. Ford (Boston, 1958), p. 9.

3. All subsequent references to the *Autobiography* will be made parenthetically following the material cited.

4. Another discussion of Mill's attitude toward this general or generic English "shame" may be found in the *Autobiography,* p. 91.

5. The *Autobiography* contains numerous other examples of the discourse of denial which I have discussed above: see pp. 5, 6, 9, 13–16, 22–23, 34, 40, 54–55, 61–62, 130. Important, too, are certain of Mill's early versions of this material; see especially *Early Draft,* pp. 179–86.

6. See *Early Draft,* pp. 13, 15, 36, 56n., 66, 69n., 181, 183, 184.

7. Mill's comments testify to another source of confusion and anger. We shall not fail to note that it is the largeness of his family to which he seemed particularly to have objected. Mill believed, it appears, that his parents' parenting—and their lovemaking—ought to have ceased "as a matter of good sense and of duty" after his own birth (Mill was his parents' eldest child). In effect he is asking: What more could my parents, especially my father, have wanted or needed once I had come into existence? Why did my parents love one another? Why did they need other children to love? Many other eldest children experience this kind of bewilderment and resentment. In Mill's instance, however, the common consciousness seems to have acquired extreme intensity and painfulness.

8. At an earlier point in the essay I suggested that one of Mill's most distressing confusions concerned the matter of his father's attitude toward the act of writing. I remarked that Mill felt mystified and terrified by his inability to distinguish himself from his parents' books— especially from the *History of British India*. We should not minimize the importance of the fact that in the *Autobiography*, Mill symbolically transformed himself into a book. Another of the subconsious compensations that Mill received from writing the *Autobiography* may have been that converting himself into a writing allowed him figuratively to become what he believed his father fundamentally wanted him to become: a text.

9. Mill, *LL*, 16: 1344.

10. I am using the phrase in the sense that Erik Erikson proposes. Erikson describes "ego identity" as a consciousness which "provides the ability to experience one's self as something that has continuity and sameness, and to act accordingly" (Erikson, *Childhood and Society*, p. 38). A. Suslick describes this awareness as "the unconscious directional pattern or sensing apparatus whereby the individual orients himself to others and to his environment. In part it consists of identifications and representations of relationships with primary love objects. . . . Ultimately it must represent a temporally persistent, co-ordinate system whereby the self is located" (Suslick, *Archives of General Psychiatry*, 8 (1963): 252.

11. Conceptions and feelings that are either "ego-dystonic" or "ego-syntonic" are materials that are either incompatible or compatible with a person's most primitive and most powerful perceptions, emotions, and needs. See Hinsie and Campbell, *Psychiatric Dictionary*, p. 257.

Chapter Seven: "One's Own Path Is Clear"

1. Mill, *LL*, 16: 1048.
2. Mill, *EL*, 12: 224.
3. Ibid., p. 161.

BIBLIOGRAPHY

I. Modern Editions

Autobiography and Other Writings. Edited by J. Stillinger. Boston: Houghton Mifflin, 1969.

Collected Works of John Stuart Mill. Edited by F. E. L. Priestley and J. M. Robson. Toronto: University of Toronto Press, 1963.

The Early Draft of John Stuart Mill's "Autobiography." Edited by J. Stillinger. Urbana: University of Illinois Press, 1961.

Essays on Politics and Culture. Edited by Gertrude Himmelfarb. Garden City: Doubleday & Co., 1962.

James and John Stuart Mill on Education. Edited by F. A. Cavenagh. Cambridge: Cambridge University Press, 1931.

John Mill's Boyhood Visit to France: Being a Journal and Notebook Written by John Stuart Mill in France, 1820–21. Edited by A. J. Mill. Toronto: University of Toronto Press, 1960.

The Letters of John Stuart Mill. Edited by Hugh S. R. Elliot. 2 vols. London: Longmans, Green and Co., 1910.

Mill's Essays on Literature and Society. Edited by J. B. Schneewind. New York: Collier, 1965.

On Liberty. Edited by D. Spitz. New York: Norton, 1975.
Prefaces to Liberty: Selected Writings of John Stuart Mill. Edited by
    B. Wishy. Boston: Beacon Press, 1959.

II. Biography and Criticism

Alexander, Edward. *Matthew Arnold and John Stuart Mill*. New York
    and London: Columbia University Press, 1965.
Anschutz, Richard P. *The Philosophy of J. S. Mill*. Oxford: Clarendon
    Press, 1953.
Bain, Alexander. *James Mill. A Biography*. London: Longmans, Green
    and Co., 1882.
————. *John Stuart Mill, A Criticism: with Personal Recollections*. Lon-
    don: Longmans, Green, and Co., 1882.
Berlin, Sir Isaiah. *Four Essays on Liberty*. Oxford: Oxford University
    Press, 1969.
Borchard, Ruth. *John Stuart Mill the Man*. London: Walts, 1957.
Bouton, C. W. "John Stuart Mill: On Liberty and History." *Western Po-
    litical Quarterly* 18 (1968): 569–78.
Britton, Karl. *John Stuart Mill*. Melbourne: Penguin, 1953.
Brown, D. G. "Mill on Liberty and Morality." *Philosophical Review* 81
    (1972): 133–58.
Brown, Norman O. *Life Against Death*. New York: Random House,
    1959.
Courtney, William L. *Life of John Stuart Mill*. London: W. Scott, 1889.
Cowling, Maurice. *Mill and Liberalism*. Cambridge: Cambridge Univer-
    sity Press, 1963.
Cranston, M. "J. S. Mill as a Political Philosopher." *History Today* 8
    (1958): 38–46.
Cumming, R. D. "Mill's History of His Ideas." *Journal of the History of
    Ideas* 25 (1964): 235–56.
Durham, J. "The Influence of John Stuart Mill's Mental Crisis on His
    Thoughts." *American Imago* 20 (1963): 369–84.
Erikson, Erik. *Childhood and Society*. New York: Norton, 1964.
Fox, Caroline. *Memories of Old Friends*. Edited by H. N. Pym. 2d ed.
    London: Smith, Elder & Co., 1882.
Freud, Sigmund. *Civilization and Its Discontents*. Edited and translated
    by James Strachey. New York: Norton, 1962.
————. *The Ego and the Id*. Edited by James Strachey. Translated by
    Joan Riviere. New York: Norton, 1962.

_____. *An Outline of Psychoanalysis.* Rev. ed. Edited and translated by James Strachey. New York: Norton, 1970.

Friedman, R. B. "A New Exploration of Mill's Essay *On Liberty.*" *Political Studies* 14 (1966): 281–304.

Froude, James A. *Thomas Carlyle: A History of His Life in London: 1834–1881.* 2 vols. London: Longmans, Green and Co., 1896.

Halévy, Elie. *The Growth of Philosophic Radicalism.* Translated by M. Morris. London: Faber & Faber, 1928.

Harrison, Frederic. *John Stuart Mill.* New York: Macmillan, 1896.

Hayek, Friedrich A. *John Stuart Mill and Harriet Taylor: Their Correspondence and Subsequent Marriage.* Chicago: University of Chicago Press, 1951.

Himmelfarb, Gertrude. *On Liberty and Liberalism: The Case of John Stuart Mill.* New York: Knopf, 1974.

Hinsie, Leland E. and Robert J. Campbell, eds. *Psychiatric Dictionary.* 4th ed. New York: Oxford University Press, 1976.

Holloway, H. A. "Mill's Liberty, 1859–1959." *Ethics* 71 (1961): 130–32.

Laski, Harold J. "Introduction." *The Autobiography of John Stuart Mill.* H. Milford: Oxford University Press, 1924.

Levi, A. W. "The 'Mental Crisis' of John Stuart Mill." *Psychoanalytic Review* 32 (January 1945): 86–101.

_____. "The Writing of Mill's *Autobiography.*" *Ethics* 61 (1951): 284–96.

McClosky, H. J. *John Stuart Mill: A Critical Study.* London: Macmillan, 1971.

Mahler, Margaret, et al. *The Psychological Birth of the Human Infant.* New York: Basic Books, 1975.

Malcolm, Janet. *Psychoanalysis: The Impossible Profession.* New York: Knopf, 1981.

Mazlish, Bruce. *James and John Stuart Mill.* New York: Basic Books, 1975.

Mill, A. J. "The Education of John—Some Further Evidence." *The Mill Newsletter* 11 (Winter 1976): 10–12.

Mineka, F. E. "The *Autobiography* and the Lady." *University of Toronto Quarterly* 32 (1963): 301–6.

Morley, John M. *Critical Miscellanies.* London: Macmillan, 1877.

Mueller, I. *John Stuart Mill and French Thought.* Urbana: University of Illinois Press, 1956.

Neff, Emery. *Carlyle and Mill: Mystic and Utilitarian.* New York: Columbia University Press, 1924; 2d ed., 1926.

Packe, Michael St. John. *The Life of John Stuart Mill*. London: Seckar & Warburg, 1970.

Pankhurst, Richard. *The Saint Simonians, Mill and Carlyle; A Preface to Modern Thought*. London: Sidgwick & Jackson, 1957.

Pappe, H. O. *John Stuart Mill and the Harriet Taylor Myth*. London: Cambridge University Press, 1960.

Rees, John C. *Mill and His Early Critics*. Leicester: University College of Leicester Press, 1956.

_____. "A Re-Reading of Mill on Liberty." *Political Studies* 6 (1958): 35–44.

Rinehart, K. "John Stuart Mill's *Autobiography:* Its Art and Appeal." *University of Kansas City Review* 19 (1953): 265–73.

Robson, John M. "Harriet Taylor and John Stuart Mill: Artist and Scientist." *Queen's Quarterly* 73 (1966): 167–86.

_____. *The Improvement of Mankind: The Social and Political Thought of John Stuart Mill*. Toronto: University of Toronto Press, 1968.

_____. "John Stuart Mill and Jeremy Bentham, with Some Observations on James Mill." In *Essays in English Literature . . . Presented to A. S. P. Woodhouse*, edited by M. MacLure and F. W. Watt, pp. 245–68. Toronto: University of Toronto Press, 1964.

_____. "Mill's *Autobiography*—the Public and Private Voice." *College Composition and Communication* 16 (1965): 97–101.

Russell, Bertrand. *Portraits from Memory*. London: Allen & Unwin, 1956.

Russell, Bertrand, and Russell, Patricia, eds. *The Amberly Papers*. 2 vols. London: Hogarth, 1937.

Ryan, A. *The Philosophy of John Stuart Mill*. London: Routledge-Kegan Paul, 1970.

Solly, H. *These Eighty Years*. 2 vols. London, 1893.

Stephen, Leslie. *The English Utilitarians*. 3 vols. London: Duckworth, 1900.

Stillinger, Jack. "Introduction." *The Autobiography of John Stuart Mill*. London: Oxford University Press, 1971.

_____. "The Text of John Stuart Mill's *Autobiography*." *Bulletin of the John Rylands Library* 43 (1960): 220–42.

Stillinger, Jack and Robson, John M. "Introduction." *Autobiography and Literary Essays, Collected Works of John Stuart Mill*. Vol. 1. Toronto: University of Toronto Press, 1981.

Street, Charles L. *Individualism and Individuality in the Philosophy of John Stuart Mill*. Milwaukee: Morehouse Publishing Co., 1926.

Ten, C. L. "Mill and Liberty." *Journal of the History of Ideas* 30 (1969): 47–68.

Ward, J. "Mill, Marx, and Modern Individualism." *Virginia Quarterly Review* 35 (1959): 527–39.

Williams, Raymond. *Culture and Society, 1780–1950* New York: Harper & Row, 1966.

Wolf, Howard R. "British Fathers and Sons, 1773–1913: From Filial Submissiveness to Creativity." *Psychoanalysis and Psychoanalytic Review* 52 (Summer 1965): 53–70.

Woods, Thomas. *Poetry and Philosophy: A Study in the Thought of John Stuart Mill.* London: Hutchinson, 1961.

INDEX

Bain, Alexander, 102, 175n.24
Bentham, Jeremy, 30, 31, 33, 34, 67–77, 78–87, 93, 157, 174n.15 *See also* Mill, John Stuart: "Bentham"; Utilitarianism
Berkeley, Bishop, 31
Boswell, James, 130
Brougham, Lord Henry, 157, 158
Brown, Norman O., 4
Brown, Thomas, 31, 79
Bulwer, Lytton, 54

Carlyle, Thomas, 28, 29, 43, 49, 50–51, 53–54, 132–33, 166, 170n.13, 172n.23, 172n.24
Coleridge, Samuel Taylor, 49, 77–87, 173n.18. *See also* Mill, John Stuart: "Coleridge"
Comte, Auguste, 49

Dickens, Charles, 2, 130, 170n.13; *Hard Times*, 128; *David Copperfield*, 137

East India Company, 171–72n.20
d'Eichthal, Gustave, 49, 51, 53
Eliot, George: *Middlemarch*, 128

Elliot, John, 109–10
Erikson, Erik, 179n.10; *Childhood and Society*, 179n.10

Forbes, Sir William, 7
Fox, R. B., 178n.9
Fox, W. J., 88
Freud, Sigmund, 21, 22, 47, 170–71n.15; *Civilization and Its Discontents*, 170–71n.15; *The Ego and the Id*, 170–71n.15
Furnivall, F. J., 90

Graham, George John, 49
Grote, Arthur, 103
Grote II, George, 31, 157, 158

Hartley, David, 31, 39
Homer: *The Odyssey*, 4, 132
Hume, David, 31, 157, 158

Levi, A. W., 39–41
Locke, John, 31, 79, 80
The London Review (*The London and Westminster Review*), 49, 54

Marmontel, Jean Francois: *Memoires d'un pere*, 38–42
Maurice, F. F., 165
Mazlish, Bruce, 175n.23, 175n.24, 177n.10
Mill, Clara, 100
Mill, Harriet Burrow (mother of John Stuart Mill), 3, 16–24, 27, 46, 48, 93, 121, 135, 141, 147-50, 152, 170n.11, 175n.23, 179n.7
Mill, Harriet Hardy Taylor (wife of John Stuart Mill), 49, 88–105, 110, 111, 121–25, 126, 135, 136, 152, 156, 158–61, 170n.7, 172n.1, 174n.6, 174n.15, 175n.23, 176n.36, 176n.44, 177n.8, 177n.10
Mill, James, 3, 7–18, 20–48, 50, 51, 52–56, 61–66, 69–77, 78–87, 90–92, 94, 100, 104, 108–10, 117–19, 121, 131, 135, 136, 140-50, 153-61, 169n.2, 170n.7, 171n.17, 171n.18, 171–72n.20, 173n.18, 174n.15, 175n.23, 175n.28, 179n.7, 179n.8, Works: *The Analysis of Pure Mind*, 79, 169n.2; *History of British India*, 140, 141, 156, 179.1
Mill, John Stuart: childhood, 1, 2–4, 7–48, 108, 119; dependency upon father, 11–16, 27–32, 39–48, 55, 61–63, 90–94, 99–101, 121–23; early education, 9–10, 58; estrangement from mother, 17–20; love, courtship, and marriage, 88–105; Oedipal hysteria, 21–24, 32–35, 40–48, 91–94, 100, 104, 142–150, 175n.23, 175n.28, 179n.7; projection of psychosexual identification onto literature, 31–32, 34–35, 87–100, 123–35, 136–63, 164–68, 176n.44; psychological crises, 35–48, 49, 53–55, 73, 102–3, 172n.21, 172n.23; resilience, xi, 3–5, 166–68; self-abnegation, 15–16, 24–30, 44–48, 150–61; separation and integration of personality, 49–66, 70–77, 84–87, 100, 104–5, 115–21, 131–35, 155, 160–63, 164–68; sublimated anger, 25, 40–48; syncretic temperament, 62–66, 69–71, 76–77, 80–87, 91–94, 97–98, 108–10, 118–19, 150, 155, 171n.18; uses and purposes of literary language, 1, 33, 44–48, 59–61, 106–10, 114–15, 117–18, 121–35, 138–40, 144–63, 164–68, 169n.3, 171–72n.20, 179n.8; tuberculosis, 96, 111. Works: *Autobiography*, 1–5, 7, 9, 10, 11, 12, 13, 14, 16, 17, 20, 24, 25, 26, 28,

29, 30, 31, 32, 33, 34, 35, 36, 37, 38, 40, 42, 43, 44, 45, 50, 70, 77, 90, 92, 93, 94, 97, 98, 103, 105, 109, 110, 121, 122, 129, 131, 132, 136–63, 178n.4, 178n.5; "Bentham," 67–77, 123, 176–77n.2; "Civilization," 55–66, 67, 75, 77, 123; "Coleridge," 77–87, 123; correspondence, 124–28; *On Liberty*, 1, 98, 105, 110–20, 121–23, 177n.10; *Principles of Political Economy*, 106, 108, 109; "The Spirit of the Age," 51–53, 77, 123; *A System of Logic*, 98,109

Nichol, John, 134
Nightingale, Florence, 155

Packe, Michael St. John, 175n.23
Priestley, Joseph, 79
Psychoanalysis, 18–22, 47, 160, 170–71n.15., 179n.10, 179n.11
Psychoanalytic criticism, ix–xi.

Reform Bill (1832), 52
Reid, Thomas, 31, 79
Ricardo, David, 157, 158
Roebuck, John Arthur, 49
Rousseau, Jean-Jacques, 163; *Confessions*,163
Ruskin, John, 170n.13

Solly, Henry, 16
Sophocles: *Oedipus the King*, 2, 132
Sterling, John, 49
Stewart, Dugald, 31, 79
Suslick, A., 179n.10

Taylor, Helen, 103
Taylor, Henry, 176n.2
Taylor, John, 88–89
Thackeray, Henry Makepeace, 170n.13
Thornton, W. T., 102
Tooke, Thomas, 49
Trollope, Anthony, 170n.13

Utilitarianism, 30–34, 61, 69–76, 80, 82, 85, 157–58, 178n.9. *See also* Bentham, Jeremy; Mill, John Stuart: "Bentham"

Victorian age, 5, 48, 51–53, 57–58, 66, 67, 69, 88, 112–13, 168, 170n.13, 178n.9. *See also* Mill, John Stuart: "The Spirit of the Age"; "Civilization"; "Bentham"; "Coleridge"; *On Liberty*

Woolf, Howard R., 177n.10
Wordsworth, William, 46, 49, 163; *The Prelude*, 163